ENGLISH ELECTRIC
CLASS 50

1967 onwards (all models)

© Jarrod Cotter 2017

First published in December 2017

A catalogue record for this book is available from the British Library.

ISBN 978 1 78521 060 0

Library of Congress control no. 2016959358

Published by Haynes Publishing,
Sparkford, Yeovil, Somerset BA22 7JJ, UK.
Tel: 01963 440635
Int. tel: +44 1963 440635
Website: www.haynes.com

Haynes North America Inc.,
859 Lawrence Drive, Newbury Park,
California 91320, USA.

Printed in Malaysia.

ENGLISH ELECTRIC
CLASS 50

1967 onwards (all models)

Owners' Workshop Manual

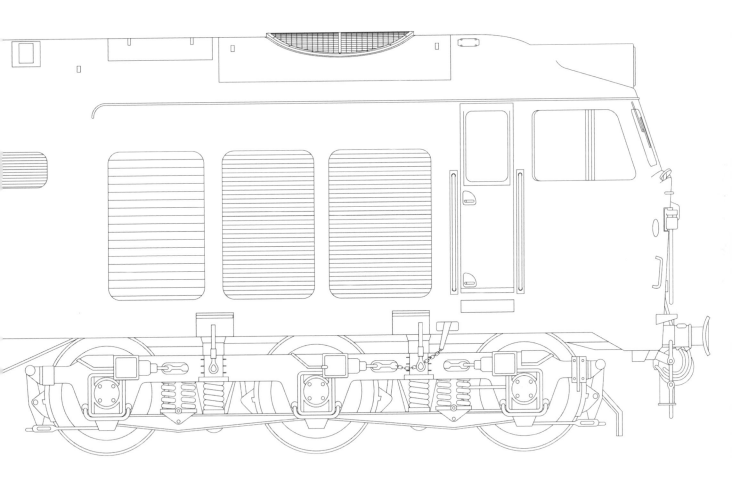

An insight into the design, construction, operation and maintenance of the classic BR diesel-electric locomotive

Jarrod Cotter

Contents

OPPOSITE No. 50049 *Defiance* on display at the Old Oak Common open day on 2 September 2017.

Foreword

It is 50 years since the class was introduced back in 1967, and 25 years since the last members of the class were retired from service with British Rail (BR) in 1992. So this makes 2017 an important year in the history of Class 50s.

By 1967, electrification of the West Coast Main Line (WCML) was progressing and had reached as far north as Crewe. There was a need for a powerful diesel locomotive to take services northward to Scotland, and to climb the formidable banks of Shap and Beattock. This resulted in the introduction of the then English Electric Type 4, D400 class (later Class 50), which often worked in multiple on Anglo-Scottish services.

The Class 50s were the last batch of first-generation diesel-electric locomotives introduced by BR in the transition from steam to diesel traction. They were designed by committee and in an attempt to build on the experience of earlier classes, included a host of new gadgets which were aimed at improving performance and reliability. Unfortunately, this was not entirely successful and in the late 1970s they underwent a refurbishment and simplification programme. This book not only traces the history of these charismatic locomotives, but also explains in detail the complexity of their design and operation.

My first acquaintance with the class was back in the summer of 1969 while staying with relatives in Penrith. One day, I was standing beside Scout Green signal box on Shap Bank when a pair of them thundered down the bank at high speed on an up express. The sight of these gleaming machines was to leave a lasting impression.

My professional involvement with the class began in 1974 when as an Engineering Trainee, I was seconded to Bath Road Depot in Bristol. The class had recently been transferred to the Western Region and I was to spend a fascinating time learning about the mystique and complexity of their electronic traction control, load-banking locomotives, and rode on them in service while fault-finding.

In 1989, I was appointed as Area Fleet Manager at Laira Traction Depot in Plymouth, where the majority of the class was now allocated. I was to oversee their final years in service and gradual withdrawal, and in many cases, transfer into preservation. The final revenue-earning service came in 1992, although three locomotives were retained until 1994 for special traffic duties.

The class has always attracted a strong following and 17 of the 50 locomotives built still survive in preservation. They have now spent as long in preservation as they had in service with British Rail. Some have even been upgraded to current standards and are certified for operation on the main line.

From a personal viewpoint I believe the Class 50s made a significant contribution to the development of diesel traction on Britain's railways and paved the way for development of probably the most successful diesel-electric 'locomotive', the HST Power Car, which after 40 years in service, is still in front-line operation and is set to continue.

Class 50s were hard work for both the staff and managers who had to try to provide a reliable service whilst controlling the unpredictable cost of their operation. They did, however, have a sense of mystique and character, and provided a sense of pride and fun to all those railwaymen who worked with them.

Geoff Hudson
Area Fleet Manager
Plymouth, 1989–96

OPPOSITE Geoff Hudson, Area Fleet Manager, Laira Depot, poses with No. **50007** *Sir Edward Elgar* in the sunshine during loco servicing at Long Rock, Penzance, on 26 March 1994. This is when the Class 50s bowed out of BR service by running the '50 Terminator' railtour from Waterloo to Penzance, then the Penzance–Paddington return. *(Paul Furtek)*

Introduction

The English Electric Type 4,
Class 50, entered service with
British Rail in October 1967. They
were the first locomotives to be
delivered in the then new BR
Rail blue livery. Fifty years later,
it has the status of being one of
the most popular diesel-electric
locomotive types ever, and can
boast an almost 'cult' following of
enthusiasts.

OPPOSITE During the early 1990s, Class 50 pioneer No. D400
was restored courtesy of a voluntary fund-raising campaign
by readers of *RAIL* magazine. It is seen here resplendent in BR
blue livery on 15 September 1991, ready for the Laira depot
open day.

ABOVE A simply charming picture. An older sister points out a Class 50-hauled train to her younger brother on Kenilworth Common on 19 August 1980, the loco in charge being No. 50009 *Conqueror.* The train was the 13.50 Paddington–Liverpool. Perhaps he went on to become a Class 50 enthusiast?

I suppose, really, growing up in a town through which the Midland Main Line ran, I should be a fan of the Class 45. Until the High Speed Train was introduced to the route in the early 1980s, it was a case of 'Peak' after 'Peak' after 'Peak'!

My interest in things with big and powerful engines began in the 1970s, and the railway was the most readily available source of such a machine. However, the monotony of seeing the same type of locomotive day after day was often frustrating, and one day while out shopping, I caught sight of an interesting book of diesel locomotives. As I turned the pages I came to a rather brilliant study of a Class 50, and caught at such a perfect angle in bright sunlight, it showed the locomotive's clean lines to such good advantage that I immediately became drawn to the type.

I wasn't really just drawn though, I became obsessed! Then, when I first saw a picture of a 50 in the then new BR large-logo livery, which I thought transformed the plain BR blue look

into something quite special, I knew that I had chosen the right class to follow.

Not only do 50s look right, they sound right too. Hearing the unmistakable English Electric 16CSVT pounding away at full chat on one of the Devon banks is a great treat.

As the railways in Britain approached privatisation, the 50s were already well on their way out. After a series of special railtours in March 1993, the surviving members of the class were confined to private, preserved railways with strictly controlled speed limits – or were they?

At The Fifty Fund's 1997 shareholders' AGM it was announced that an opportunity for main line running had arisen. Little did most there realise that before the year was out, No. 50031 *Hood* would be once again storming up Hemerdon with a load of 12 on! On 1 November 1997, just over four years since withdrawal, the Class 50 had returned to the main line by hauling 'The Pilgrim Hoover' railtour!

Having put together a number of Haynes Owners' Workshop Manuals on aircraft, including the iconic Avro Lancaster, I knew that the format of these books could work well for railway locomotives and therefore offered the idea of a Class 50 Manual. What else! The historic story of the Class 50 has been told many times, so in this book I haven't gone into great detail regarding that aspect; I have instead just picked out the main highlights. The idea of these books is to

offer a completely new look at their subject, with an unusual variety of topics covered.

During my research I was very lucky to unearth two 'long-lost' documents from the late 1960s, which I think add a fascinating element to the contents. Both of these were preliminary documents, one covering driving instructions as per 1967, and the other covering the electronic

equipment with hand-written amendments by Crewe electricians that had been made in 1969.

There is also vital input from some of the well-known names in the Class 50 world, both with BR and in preservation. My special thanks go to Geoff Hudson for offering to write a foreword. As you will all know, Geoff had the unenviable task of overseeing the withdrawal of the 50s while he

ABOVE The author is visible here in the secondman's seat of the No. 2 leading end of No. 50033 *Glorious* on this visit by the then National Railway Museum Class 50 to the East Lancashire Railway. He had long wanted a cab ride in *Glorious*, and when this picture appeared in the *ELR News* he contacted the photographer to ask for a copy, and he kindly obliged! *(Peter Marsh)*

LEFT When producing a book on any subject, finding long-lost documents relating to it are worth their weight in gold to an author. Therefore, obtaining these two rather sorry-looking pieces of history was a most fortunate coup for the author.

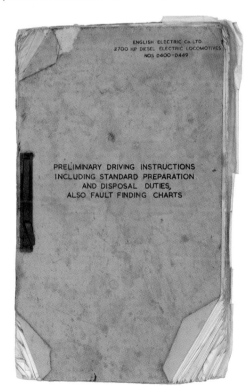

ENGLISH ELECTRIC Co. LTD
2700 HP DIESEL ELECTRIC LOCOMOTIVES
NOS D400-D449

PRELIMINARY DRIVING INSTRUCTIONS
INCLUDING STANDARD PREPARATION
AND DISPOSAL DUTIES,
ALSO FAULT FINDING CHARTS

C.M.E.E. TRAINING UNIT
LONDON ROAD
DERBY

CREWE

D.400,
**ELECTRONIC EQUIPMENT
DIESEL – ELECTRIC LOCOMOTIVES**

NOVEMBER 1969

A close-up of the cast brass BR double arrows and LA Laira lettering on the cabside front of the No. 2 end of No. 50007 *Sir Edward Elgar*. After its transformation into Great Western green in 1984 this loco became a celebrity and a firm favourite with both enthusiasts and railwaymen. When asked, most who retired from Laira requested a photograph of this loco.

LEFT In this view of No. 50042 *Triumph* on the Bodmin & Wenford Railway, the author is seen leaning out of the driver's window of the No. 1 end during a driver experience course in 1993.

was the Area Fleet Manager at Plymouth Laira Depot, but he did a really splendid job of it and made sure they went out in style.

Geoff was also instrumental in making sure the withdrawal of the Class 50s was recorded on camera in a way that no other class had ever been treated before.

Of course, this book was deliberately planned for first publication on the 50th anniversary of the Class 50s entering service with BR. So I hope that it marks that occasion in fitting style, offering readers a completely new look at the class, with the majority of photographs being previously unpublished.

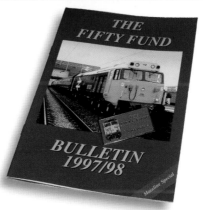

THE
FIFTY FUND

BULLETIN
1997/98

Mainline Special

LEFT The author is a shareholder in The Fifty Fund, and here is his shareholder's badge on top of the 1997/98 Mainline Special of the Fund's Bulletin.

RIGHT In the 1970s, if you wanted value-for-money Class 50 haulage this was the way to do it! If you could afford the long journey from most parts of the country to Plymouth, for just £5.75 more you could get a week's Runabout season ticket from there, westwards. This meant you could travel behind all the Class 50s in Cornwall, after 08.30, from Monday to Friday and all weekend! Just think about that, and compare it to nowadays with the type of trains available to travel on, and also take into account the prolifically higher capacity timetable that was running in the 1970s and '80s. Happy days indeed...

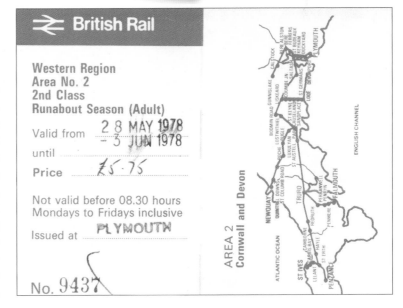

British Rail

Western Region
Area No. 2
2nd Class
Runabout Season (Adult)

Valid from   2 8 MAY 1978
              - 3 JUN 1978
until
Price   £5.75

Not valid before 08.30 hours
Mondays to Fridays inclusive
Issued at   PLYMOUTH

No. 9437

AREA 2
Cornwall and Devon

Chapter One

The Class 50 story

Originally operating on the London Midland Region of British Railways at a time when main line steam locomotives were rapidly being withdrawn and the West Coast Main Line (WCML) was being fully electrified, the 50 brand-new Class 50s provided a lifeline in terms of motive power. However, it was when they later transferred to the Western Region that these stylish diesel-electrics found popularity and their true home.

OPPOSITE The author is openly claiming this to be one of the most perfect photographs of a Class 50 ever taken! It shows No. 50043 *Eagle* at Hereford in October 1984. Any challenging pictures would be greatly welcomed!

The English Electric Company's (EE) first venture into diesel rail traction came in 1927 when it produced the electrical equipment for a diesel railcar built by the London, Midland & Scottish Railway (LMS). Then, in 1934, the company produced the K model diesel engine of which a six-cylinder version, the 6KT, was used for the LMS's 350bhp 0-6-0 shunters.

Later developments of this engine included a 16-cylinder variant, the 16SVT, and this was used in the first main line diesel locomotive to run on Britain's railways, LMS No. 10000 which emerged from Derby Works on 8 December 1947. No. 10000 was joined by No. 10001 in July the following year, following Nationalisation of the railways.

EE also provided an even more powerful version of the 16SVT engine and many main components for the Southern prototypes, Nos 10201, 10202 and 10203, the first of which was completed at Ashford Works in December 1950.

When the British Transport Commission (BTC) announced its Pilot Scheme for the replacement of steam locomotives, the relative success of the early prototypes made EE an obvious choice to supply new types. EE's first diesel locomotives for BR were the Type 1 Class 20 (1957) and the Type 4 Class 40 (1958), which were fitted with 8- and 16-cylinder versions of the MkII SVT engine respectively. In January 1959, the BTC ordered a new medium-power Type 3 locomotive from EE, which appeared in the form of the ubiquitous Class 37, the first of which was delivered in December 1960. EE also developed the iconic Class 55 'Deltics', 22 of which were produced in 1961 and 1962.

DP2

Earlier, in January 1960, the BTC had announced it required a new, large Type 4 diesel-electric locomotive, fitted with an engine capable of producing 2,700bhp. By May 1961, EE was working on a design to meet this requirement, although the company was at the same time concentrating heavily on producing the 'Deltics'. However, the same month the company unveiled its 16-cylinder 16CSVT engine, which could provide the required 2,700bhp at 167hp per cylinder. In order to test the engine, EE decided the quickest and cheapest solution would be to fit the new engine in a Class 55 bodyshell.

No. DP2 first appeared on the BR network in May 1962, and along with its bodyshell, most of its superstructure was identical to a 'Deltic'. The loco was initially turned out in an all-over dark green livery, which was later changed to the BR two-tone green of the time. On 2 May 1962, it made a proving run from its birthplace at Vulcan Foundry, Newton-le-Willows, to Chester and return. Then, on the 8th, DP2 hauled a test train from Crewe to Penrith and return. Following crew training the loco began hauling scheduled services from 14

BELOW The test bed for the new equipment to be used on the Type 4 Class 50 was DP2, which for ease of build, utilised a Class 55 'Deltic' bodyshell. *(Colour Rail)*

May, initially between London Euston and Liverpool Lime Street. DP2 took up Euston–Carlisle turns later in the year, and from summer 1963 it was transferred to the Eastern Region taking up 'Deltic' duties out of King's Cross.

In 1965, BR ordered a fleet of 50 Type 4s of a new design from EE, which was to feature the BTC's new requirement for a flat cab front. DP2 was to act as a test bed for the electronic control system which was going to be used in the new design, and so the loco was taken out of service on 31 January 1966 for the installation of this equipment. It was then utilised on various services as well as trials for the new slow-speed control system for the working of merry-go-round coal trains.

On 31 July 1967, it was heading north out of York en route for Edinburgh when it collided with some derailed freight wagons, causing severe damage. DP2 was considered for repair, but this was never carried out and it languished at Vulcan Foundry until 1970 when parts were recovered for the new Type 4 fleet for which it had acted as the pioneer.

DP2 had travelled just over 607,000 miles in its short life, which, even though an EE engineer always travelled on board to rectify any technical issues which could be fixed locally while out and about, was quite an exceptional figure to reach.

Enter the Class 50

With the incomplete signalling of the WCML there was a requirement for a minimum of 50 Type 4 diesel locomotives, but more powerful than the 2,000bhp Class 40s, so these would be based on something similar to the Brush Type 4 design (Class 47).

At the time, BR's finances were restricted, and realising this, EE instead offered to build and lease a fleet of Type 4s in order to make securing an order more likely. EE further sweetened the deal by including an availability guarantee of 42 locomotives being serviceable each day, with a penalty payable to BR if that figure was not available for traffic.

BR agreed to this attractive deal in November 1965 and EE contract CCT1421 which later specified the construction of 50 100mph Type 4 locomotives. It was also a

ABOVE **DP2 awaits departure from King's Cross, where to the untrained eye, it would have appeared to be just another Class 55 'Deltic'.** (English Electric)

BELOW **A frame laid ready for Class 50 production at Newton-le-Willows, Lancashire. The initial fitting was carried out with the frame inverted.** (English Electric)

RIGHT Multiple Class 50 production underway at Vulcan Foundry, Newton-le-Willows in early 1968. *(English Electric)*

BELOW A 16CSVT engine being lowered into a Class 50 during production at Vulcan Foundry in 1968. *(English Electric)*

BELOW RIGHT An almost complete No. D437 seen inside the main construction shop at Vulcan Foundry in mid-1968. *(English Electric)*

milestone in BR history in that these locos would be delivered in the then-new BR all-over Rail blue livery with white double-arrow logos.

The first two locomotives were initially planned to be handed over to BR in July 1967, and production was then to rise to five per month with a delivery completion date for the whole fleet of June 1968. This later changed to a first delivery in August 1967, and No. D400's engine was tested early that month. However, the engine was running hot so possible cures for this were investigated and the pioneer Class 50 moved under its own power for the first time on 19 August. BR staff were at Vulcan Works to check on the testing of the loco with No. D400 passed as fit to run on the BR network on 4 September 1967. It made a light engine test run to Chester and return on the 11th. The following day, it made two return trips from Crewe to Stafford with 15 coaches in

RIGHT **An English Electric leasing plate as applied to Class 50s in their early years.**
(UK Railwayana)

tow to test if it could reach 100mph with such a load. It did, but apparently only just. On 13 September, D400 was really put to the test with a maximum-load trial over Shap and Beattock with a 1,000-ton oil train in tow. Further commissioning tests followed over the coming days and D400 returned to Vulcan Foundry for rectification work on the 22nd.

Following this, five days later, the loco went to Crewe and on 5 October was put to the test for a final commissioning report, on a return run to Carlisle heading 17 coaches. Train heat was used for 30 minutes during the run and although a few more minor problems had arisen, BR issued an acceptance certificate with D400 declared available for driver and depot staff training.

The first proper use of the Class 50s on which BR put them to work was the Crewe–Perth segments of trains out of Euston. With the number of Class 50s in traffic rising, by the end of February 1968 they were put in charge of other Anglo–Scottish services, including most notably, trains to Glasgow. They were also used on a large amount of LMR freight work.

ABOVE Bowler-hatted Chief Traction Inspector John Hughes checks for a clear road ahead as the pioneer Class 50, No. D400, makes its debut in October 1967, emerging from Vulcan Foundry and running on to BR rails for the first time. *(E.N. Bayliss)*

LEFT No. D437 as it appeared ex-works for a press photograph in September 1968. *(British Railways)*

Double-heading and TOPS

New timetables and track rationalisation in early 1970 resulted in London–Glasgow trains being scheduled to take considerably less time to make the journey. If locomotives were to achieve this speeding-up of the trains they would be hauling, then either the loads would need to be reduced or more power would be required.

As the Class 50s had been designed with

LEFT In 1967, when the Class 50s were introduced, the electrification of the West Coast Main Line had reached as far as Crewe, where electric locomotive Class 86 No. E3157 is seen waiting to be detached from the 1S75 service.

LEFT A double-headed Class 50-hauled train led by No. 50035 awaits to take 1S75 northwards. *(David N. Clough)*

BELOW LEFT Double-headed Nos D435 and D436 take a service northwards out of Crewe towards the yet-to-be-electrified portion of the West Coast Main Line, in the late 1960s.

BELOW The cover of the 1967 *British Railways Working Instructions for A.C. Electrified Lines*.

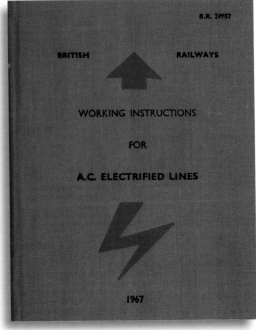

B.R. 29987

BRITISH   RAILWAYS

WORKING INSTRUCTIONS

FOR

A.C. ELECTRIFIED LINES

1967

RIGHT Having lost its 'D' prefix, No. 444 heads north with its consist out of Crewe during the late 1960s.

multiple-unit jumper capability (only No. D400 had been delivered with the external equipment fitted), they offered the relatively simple solution of working in pairs while in charge of the premier services. Therefore, from the summer 1970 timetable, principal Anglo–Scottish services were scheduled for pairs of Class 50s. In order to facilitate this requirement, the whole fleet was fitted with the multiple jumper cables in early 1970 to match that of D400.

With the rapidly extending electrification of the WCML, reallocation of the Class 50s to the Western Region began in October 1972, and that is covered in the next section.

From 6 June 1973, BR began its TOPS (Total Operations Processing System) renumbering and classification of its entire fleet of locomotive classes. It was only now that the English Electric Type 4 (Nos D400 to D449) became known as Class 50 and were renumbered in the 500xx series. The first to be so renumbered was D426, which became 50026 on 29 July 1973. The last was D413, which became 50013 on 19 June 1974. The first, No. D400, became No. 50050 as the TOPS series always started at '001, not '000.

DANGER

OVERHEAD LIVE WIRES

LEFT An early variant of the 'Danger – Overhead Live Wires' warning signs that were attached to locomotives.

BELOW A classic scene from the late 1960s as a pair of unidentified Class 50s cross Ribblehead Viaduct with a northbound passenger working on the Settle and Carlisle line.

ABOVE The Class 50 was a mixed-traffic locomotive and here, No. 50040 is seen in charge of an empty car transporter train.

BELOW After May 1974, the LMR made use of the Class 50's slow-speed control capability on merry-go-round (mgr) coal work when a Class 47 was not available. Seen here on 15 August 1974 is No. 50035 heading towards Newton-le-Willows with the 10.13 from Bickershaw Colliery to Fiddler's Ferry Power Station. (David N. Clough)

In early 1974, BR bought the Class 50 fleet from English Electric. From May that year, the LMR had just 15 of the class remaining on its books, and the locos had reverted to working singly. During this period, with the LMR Class 50s becoming frequent motive power of merry-go-round coal trains, their slow-speed control could be put to use. All members of the class had been transferred to the WR by the end of 1976.

On the Western Region

While the Class 50s had begun their career on the LMR, it was on the Western Region where the type was to really find its niche. On the WCML unreliability had constantly caused concerns, but they were considered to be only an interim measure until full electrification of that route was achieved. They were therefore initially regarded with some scepticism by the WR on arrival.

The National Traction Plan had sealed the fate of the non-standard diesel-hydraulics on the WR, and the last to be replaced were the popular Class 52 'Westerns'. BR decided the Class 50s could take on some of their turns as they were capable of hauling express passenger trains at 100mph.

This inevitably meant the Class 50s were initially very unpopular with the diesel-hydraulic aficionados, which as well as railway enthusiasts, also included drivers and engineers! However, it is published in numerous sources that it was the proposed introduction of High Speed Trains (HSTs), the InterCity 125, which actually saw the end of the 'Westerns', not the Class 50.

Reallocation of all Class 50s to the WR had begun in October 1972 when the first-built locomotive, No. D400, was sent to Bristol Bath Road for driver training. A 50 first arrived at Paddington on 1 December 1972, while the type's first use hauling a scheduled train from Paddington occurred on 15 January 1973, when D400 had charge of the 17.12 to Weston-super-Mare.

It is said that it was staff at Paddington who

LEFT An unrefurbished No. 50042 stabled by Old Oak Common's turntable.

gave the class its 'Hoover' nickname, as the sound made by the locos at rest was likened to the products of the famous manufacturer of vacuum cleaners.

More 50s soon followed No. D400 to the WR, and the pioneer member of the fleet was then sent further south-west to be based at Plymouth Laira. Former Laira fitter, Mike Woodhouse, described the arrival in this extract from his book of memoirs, *Blood, Sweat and Fifties,* published in 1990:

"Anyone who has worked for British Rail over the last 25 years will have seen many changes in the locomotive fleet. Enginemen, engineers and management alike have had to adapt – particularly so if you were a Western Region man. This region of the BR system has always been different from the rest, not least its adoption of diesel-hydraulic traction, whereas the others went straight from steam to diesel-electric. Even today some claim the Western made the right choice.

"Laira depot, at Plymouth in the heart of the Western Region, has likewise seen many changes. It was one of the first diesel depots to be completed in the country, and it is also the only one to have been home to seven varieties of Type 4 locomotive, though not all at the same time. For the record these were Classes 41/42/43/46/47/50/52. The last to arrive was, of course, the Class 50.

"Outside the old servicing shed (where the new HST depot has since been built) there was a short loco spur known as the sand road. It was normally used by visiting motive power or failures. A further use was to accommodate new types being used for train crew and workshop familiarisation. At this time the elimination of the hydraulics was in progress; the last 63xx out of Swindon, 6319, was already laid up. Replacement for the Type 2s, the Class 25 diesel-electric, was represented by 5179 in use for crew training purposes. 5827 soon followed, still in green with double white arrows.

"It was in 1973 when another stranger was due to come west, this time as a replacement for the Class 52 'Westerns'. Enter the English Electric Class 50, or D400s as they were in the original numbering. D400 first visited Laira in July 1973, on loan from Bristol Bath Road for both driver and engineer training. It reposed on the sand road and over the following months

was swapped several times for 401, minus its D prefix. After one such changeover 400 returned as 50050. D402 had been visiting Old Oak Common for the same reason.

"It takes time to adjust to change, and when staff learned that the D400s were to replace our trusty 1000s they were not happy. Officially it was put across that the new type would be trouble-free and require less maintenance. Unofficially staff heard the LMR would be glad to see the back of them, and this did not help in the adjustment. Our first impressions confirmed why they were not wanted in the North: the interiors were filthy, and were no place for crawling around in like monkeys whilst fault-finding. The inertia (non) filters were particularly bad. Another feature we did not like was that the door handles moved up to open the door, not downwards as on other types, which is so much easier when your hands are full of tools and a hand lamp. This would not have been too bad but there were so many internal doors and the interior lighting was poor.

"To the electricians they were a nightmare. Although we did have a few diesel-electrics

ABOVE No. 50046, by-then named *Ajax*, runs through Reading in unrefurbished and a rather work-stained condition on 9 April 1981.

BELOW Refurbished No. 50013 *Agincourt* is seen at Plymouth Laira. This was the sixth Class 50 to undergo the refurbishment programme and was completed on 26 June 1980.

ABOVE Unrefurbished Class 50 pioneer No. 50050 (ex-No. D400) stands at Exeter St David's. This loco is instantly identifiable as it is the only member of the class which lacks handrails on its face, below the main windscreen panels.

also had to be understood. No-one at Laira had much knowledge of electronics on locos at the time, and so the CM&EE's representatives had to help out with repairs.

"On the other hand, the train crews certainly liked them on first impressions. To the drivers they were fast and powerful and they also rode well. Unlike the 'Westerns', though, which had double bulkheads between driver and engines, they were noisier and less comfortable in the cabs and the seats were set too low.

"The first allocation of a Class 50 at Laira was 50003 at the start of April 1974. At this stage many of the depot staff shied away from working on the new locos, preferring to stick to the familiar 'Westerns'. It was not surprising that the feeling towards the EE Type 4s was 'give us a Class 52 any day'. On arrival, 50003 required a 'D' exam, which is quite an in-depth maintenance programme. This would really test staff knowledge of how the loco worked! 50003 was berthed on No. 6 road against the stop blocks – and seemed to stay there for ages, whilst several 52s were called in for the exam and returned back to traffic. I began to wonder if the Fifty would ever turn a wheel again, the old joke for locos like this being to put grass cuttings under the wheels. But to be fair, all the staff had to start from scratch in getting to grips with these maintenance schedules, finding the right location on the loco, and then working out the best way of tackling the various jobs in practice. The management were in the dark, and the stores supply was nil – parts having to be requested from Crewe, Bath Road or Old Oak.

"As more of the class came to the Western more problems came to light, the dynamic braking system becoming a particular headache. But as always the Western found its own solutions, including the refurbishment programme of the early 1980s.

"With the timetable changes in May 1990, Laira was home to all of the remaining Class 50s."

End-to-end

The first WR diagram of the Class 50 occurred in August 1973, when the Monday to Friday 08.05 and 15.15 Bristol–Paddington and 11.45 and 18.45 returns were scheduled. The first

BELOW No. 50012 is seen shunting between trains at Penzance on a sunny day in 1976. The first Class 50 to arrive at Penzance was No. D427, which reached this furthest west destination of the Western Region on 19 March 1974.

already, the 25s and 46s, compared to a hydraulic which only had pump failure and earth faults to be dealt with, the 50s were something different. There was an electronic control system instead of the older style electro-mechanical or pneumatic, plus subsystems for slow speed control, current limiting and rheostatic braking. I remember spending a day on this braking system, the ultimate in braking, only fitted to this diesel class. The main generators and traction motors

Class 50 to arrive at Penzance in Cornwall was D427, which reached this furthest destination of the WR on 19 March 1974. In their heyday the Class 50s became synonymous with running between Paddington and Penzance, these two famous termini being 305¼ miles apart.

As the year progressed more Class 50s were sent west. From the start of the summer 1974 timetable they were the primary motive power on London–Bristol trains.

Just as the Class 50s had replaced the 'Westerns', it was not long before the new Type 4's operations began to be threatened by the intended introduction of the HST. However, it was to go on to be a stalwart of WR trains before then.

Even the famous 'Cornish Riviera' and 'Night Riviera' trains began to be hauled by Class 50s. These were premier day and night trains running from London Paddington to Penzance, and still run under the same names to this day. At one point during its very early running, the first scheduled stop for the 'Cornish Riviera' was St Erth, deep into Cornwall, and the station from where passengers alight to change for the St Ives branch to visit one of the county's most popular holiday destinations.

The type continued on London commuter services from Paddington to the West Country and had for some years found great acclaim with enthusiasts on Plymouth–Penzance 'locals'. With just four or five coaches in tow these powerful locomotives plied their trade on the picturesque Cornish main line, Plymouth being literally just over the county border into Devon.

Refurbishment

It was during the Class 50's time on the Western Region that the locomotives received the names of warships. The first to be so named was No. 50035, which gained the name *Ark Royal* on 17 January 1978. It also received large twinning crests with the Royal Navy ship, which were placed above the nameplate for a ceremony at Plymouth North Road station.

HSTs were due to take over principal services from May 1980, although technical problems delayed this for a while, and Class 50s were called upon regularly to deputise. At around this time the Class 50s were also undergoing refurbishment at Doncaster Works to improve their reliability.

Many problems had been encountered with the LMR and these continued on the WR, with faults ranging from minor electrical malfunctions to serious component failures. In 1973, BR and EE began to seriously try to eradicate these problems, but availability figures did not improve. In the coming years the miles per casualty figure fell to around 8,500, and by the time of the 1979 WR traction planning, availability had dropped to just 55%.

The WR engineers tried to improve figures by

BELOW No. 50006 *Neptune* departs from Newton Abbot with a westbound service *c*1980.

ABOVE Seen thundering along the picturesque Dawlish sea wall on 28 August 1980 is No. 50020 *Revenge.*

putting in place a 'make-simple' maintenance policy where much of the troublesome electronic-based systems causing problems were isolated, including the slow-speed control, the rheostatic brakes, and automatic wheelslip correction systems.

Availability did improve slightly, but in 1977, a major initiative by the WR into Class 50 failures was launched. This recommended a major series of modifications if availability figures were to be improved. This work, required for all 50 Class 50s, was beyond the scope of Laira and would also be very costly and therefore far above the routine repair/maintenance budget.

BELOW No. 50005 *Collingwood* storms past the camera near Bromsgrove on 3 June 1981.

Authorisation was given to refurbish the fleet and the M&EE Department at the Derby RTC commenced detailed planning with BREL Doncaster, which was by then responsible for major overhauls of the 50s. By early 1978, planning was at a stage where modified electrical equipment was installed in No. 50016. The refurbishment programme was defined by the end of the year and No. 50006, which had been at Doncaster since September, was chosen as the first member of the fleet to have this major work carried out, this beginning in early 1979. The main aspects of the refurbishment programme can be summarised as follows:

- The installation of a new air management and primary filtration system, which would incorporate 41 filter panels.
- The modification to the clean air compartment (No. 1 end) by the installation of six dry pack filter panels in two banks.
- Major alterations to the No. 2 end air filtration compartment including panelling over the former lower roof cut-out section, and the installation of a new angle air filtration system in the position of the former rheostatic brake equipment. The air filters were supplied by Vokes and were of similar style to those already used for HST power cars.
- The alteration of the compartment layout at No. 2 end with the removal of the engine room circulation bulkhead and the installation of an additional bulkhead between the power unit and generator group to prevent the air for the generator being contaminated with oil and dirt.
- Modification to the ventilation of the engine room by the fitting of a scavenger fan and

ABOVE An unrefurbished No. 50044 *Exeter* awaits departure from Exeter St David's c1980.

ABOVE RIGHT No. 50045 *Achilles* leads an unidentified 50 out of Newton Abbot on a westbound double-header.

RIGHT A sunny, early morning scene at Penzance in the late 1970s, as a Class 50 awaits departure from Platform 1 with an up service.

roof extractor to induce the air flow through the No. 1 end side louvre (former window), past the power unit and out via the roof vent. This additional fan was to be powered by a small motor fed from the auxiliary generator.

■ Elimination of the redundant weight transfer equipment.

■ Modification to the engine spillage tank and fitting of an 88 gallon capacity retention unit.

■ Full refurbishment of all electrical equipment including complete rewiring.

■ Removal of the redundant sand equipment and the panelling over of filler ports.

■ Rewinding of the main generator, auxiliary generator and traction motors.

RIGHT With No. 50017 *Royal Oak* nearest the camera, a pair of Class 50s bask in the sunshine at Old Oak Common. *Royal Oak* is fitted with a high-intensity headlight.

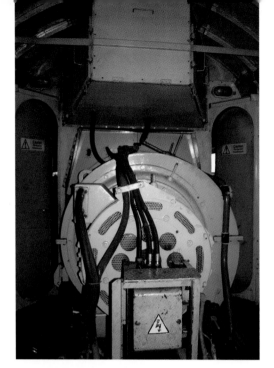

■ Re-routing of under-floor cables into new trunking routes.

■ Modifications to the radiator fan speed control system.

■ The installation of a high-intensity headlight in the centre of the locomotive's front ends.

■ The reduction of cab controls by removing any unneeded equipment.

■ The refurbishment was to include a major classified overhaul on each item of equipment that was removed as part of the process.

The refurbishment of No. 50006 was obviously also to act as a trial for the BREL Doncaster staff who were working on equipment that was unfamiliar to them, but who would be required to carry out the work on another 49 locomotives. As they learned along the way, the staff managed to reduce the timescale for the refurbishment of subsequent locomotives and which was amended along the way to make further improvements.

Varied services

With their improved reliability the Class 50s became the staple power for overnight services from Paddington to the West Country until Sectorisation. They were also a common sight at Paddington and Penzance on parcel and newspaper vans, both by day and by night. The type even hauled the prestigious Travelling Post Office (TPO) trains into and out of Penzance.

ABOVE Complete with snowploughs fitted, No. 50037 *Illustrious* awaits departure from Paddington in February 1986. HST power car No. 253001, in original livery, is on the left.

LEFT A later variant of the 'Danger – Overhead Live Wires' warning signs as attached to locomotives.

RIGHT No. 50014 *Warspite* was the last member of the Class 50 fleet to be refurbished, being completed on 7 December 1983. It is seen here in October 1985.

BELOW No. 50022 *Anson* was the sixth Class 50 to be withdrawn, bowing out of service after an engine problem on 20 September 1988 while hauling the 11.57 Portsmouth Harbour–Plymouth. It is seen on a happier day in June 1985.

BELOW RIGHT An impressive view of No. 50029 *Renown* climbing away from Aller Junction with a Plymouth-bound service on 31 May 1985.

RIGHT One of the most picturesque stretches of the British railway system is the Dawlish sea wall, as typified here with No. 50039 *Implacable* in July 1985.

RIGHT No. 50048 *Dauntless* crosses Moorswater Viaduct in Cornwall on 14 September 1979.

BELOW With an impressive gantry of semaphore signals in view, No. 50031 *Hood* departs from Exeter on 21 July 1984.

BELOW RIGHT A good study of No. 50012 *Benbow* at Exeter St David's on 17 March 1982.

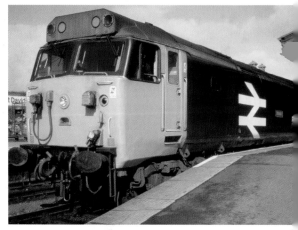

These were the up 'Great West TPO', which departed Penzance at 19.22, while running in the other direction was the 'Down Great West TPO'. By the early 1990s these trains only ran to and from Plymouth.

Another duty the 50s picked up for two years or so during the mid-1980s on the Western Region was hauling the 'Jumbo' trains. These consisted of a 13-coach load between Paddington and Penzance to relieve congestion on HSTs.

Waterloo Sunset

As the HSTs took their hold on the premier WR services the 50s began to be utilised on other routes, notably as the staple motive power on the former LSWR Waterloo–Exeter

ABOVE Complete with a distinctive Laira black roof, No. 50028 *Tiger* is caught at speed in June 1986.

LEFT Wearing original Network SouthEast (NSE) livery, No. 50044 *Exeter* runs through the attractive Sydney Gardens, Bath, in July 1986.

FAR LEFT Also in original NSE livery, No. 50018 *Resolution* waits at Exeter St David's in May 1987.

LEFT No. 50026 *Indomitable* makes a nocturnal stop at Reading's Platform 6 in December 1988.

Former Laira fitter Mike Woodhouse describes the life and times of celebrity loco No. 50007 in this extract from his 1990 book of memoirs, *Blood, Sweat and Fifties*. (See editor's note below.)

"This story concerns the third locomotive of the British Railways fleet to carry the name *Hercules*. The first was the 4-6-0 steam loco 45703 of the London Midland Region (*sic*). The second was No. D822, a Western Region hydraulic built at Swindon in 1960. Just seven years later the frames were laid at Newton-le-Willows in Lancashire for the third *Hercules*. D407 emerged anonymous, just another 100mph D400 class for use between Crewe and Scotland; but today the loco has become the flagship of the Western fleet. To paraphrase a well-known saying: 'they seek him here, they seek him there, they seek *Sir Edward Elgar* everywhere!'

"D407 was allocated from its native LMR to the WR at Laira in April 1974, one of the first to be transferred. Soon afterwards it was renumbered 50007. In 1974 it suffered serious damage to the cab at No. 1 end whilst shunting at Bristol. I can remember the managers talking to the welders and sheet metalworkers to see if Laira could undertake the repair. In the event two of my workmates proved that it could, '07 being berthed on No. 5 road stop blocks and the cab stripped out. Gradually the nose was

brought back into shape. One of our welders had worked in the RN dockyard at Devonport, and for him the work was easy when compared to patching up a ship.

"At last the work was done, this being the biggest job ever achieved on Laira depot. Even today the scars of the job can still be seen, notably on the buffer beam, but '07 still lives.

"The name *Hercules* was applied on 6 April 1978, the 11th of the class to be named. Nearly five years later the loco emerged from the refurbishment programme in the new Large Logo livery, the 35th to be treated, but was still just one of the crowd.

"1984 changed all that. Early in the year it was announced that 50007 was to be renamed *Sir Edward Elgar* and repainted in GWR Brunswick green, in connection with the 50th anniversary of the composer's death, and as a prelude to the Great Western 150th anniversary celebrations. Much controversy surrounded the move; some enthusiasts were outraged, and the affair even reached the local newspapers. Whatever the rights and wrongs (for example the appropriateness of having 49 naval 50s and one musician), the decision stood.

"The conversion process was swift, as the official naming ceremony was to take place at Paddington on 25th February. At 16.00 hours on Wednesday the 8th, '07 lost its *Hercules*

BELOW Nos 50007 *Sir Edward Elgar* and 50050 *Fearless* are seen near Exminster with the '50 Terminator' on 26 March 1994.

nameplates, to be sold at Collector's Corner in Euston. By Saturday the loco had been given a suitable undercoat for its pre-war green livery, the top coat being applied the following day, the Sunday. On Monday the roof was painted black, as were the bogies on Tuesday, and the buffer beam in red on Wednesday. The lining out was completed on Thursday the 16th, with the next three days being occupied by bogie repairs and painting the inside of the cabs. The brass GWR-style number plates were attached on the Friday and the nameplates the following Monday. After inspection the new-look '07 left Laira for Old Oak at 00.05 hours on Tuesday the 21st.

"Simon Rattle of the Birmingham Symphony Orchestra unveiled the *Sir Edward Elgar* plaques on the appointed day, which was marred only by persistent traction motor problems. Since then '07 has become very well-known, travelling the BR system to attend numerous Open Days. In 1985/6, for example, it visited Birkenhead, Canon Street, Carlisle, Coalville and Landore – to name but a few.

"In March 1987 an 'F' exam was carried out on *Sir Edward*, but the loco was not repainted. Two years later Sectorisation meant that 50007 had to join the NSSA fleet in the Network SouthEast stable, which meant that a repaint into the standard NSE livery was required. However, a decision came down from on high that a dispensation would be granted for '07 to retain its Brunswick green livery, as a special 'thank you' from Network SouthEast to the Laira staff for keeping the Fifties running. So it was that a full repaint was undertaken in

time for the 21st anniversary of the BR Staff Association club at Laira. '07 was presented back to the NSE fleet, with all staff – past and present – attending the ceremony. All the Depot Engineers from the 1960s to the 1990s helped to plant a tree of dedication.

"50007 was well and truly Laira's flagship. As a footnote, the Areat Fleet Manager [Geoff Hudson] is an ex-Eastern Region man, and so '07 carries the embellishment 'Laira' on its buffer beams – after the King's Cross 'top shed' tradition."

Editor's note: The first BR loco named Hercules *was incorrectly described in the book. It was not LMR 'Jubilee' class 4-6-0 No. 45703, which was in fact named* Thunderer (*as was Class 50 No. 50008*), *but was a former industrial railway Peckett 0-4-0ST which was absorbed by BR and given the number 1.*

TOP Nos. 50050 and 50007 after arrival at London Paddington on 26 March 1994, having worked the '50 Terminator' railtour from London Waterloo via Exeter and Penzance.

ABOVE GWR green No. 50007 *Sir Edward Elgar* at Salisbury with a rake of NSE-liveried stock.

ABOVE LEFT The positions of a Class 50's four exhaust ports can be seen in this view of No. 50004 *St Vincent* while it stands at Exeter on 24 October 1987.

ABOVE No. 50034 *Furious* storms through the London suburbs in work-worn original NSE livery.

ABOVE No. 50029 *Renown* rolls into Cardiff on 22 September 1987.

line. This was to become the last bastion for regular Class 50-hauled scheduled services, with most locomotives wearing the Network SouthEast livery of the route's operator.

This route was once pounded by the Southern prototypes Nos. 10201, 10202 and 10203, which incorporated EE equipment. In 1964,

following the last run of the line's most famous train the 'Atlantic Coast Express', the route was downgraded with stations closed and sections of line singled. This is a demanding route, but the Class 50s handled it well, and following the use of Class 42 'Warships' and later Class 33s, the 50s brought with them the fastest timings in decades. Some stations were reopened and passing loops were reinstated and it actually became a very prosperous route, and was in later years, a lifeline for the Class 50s.

RIGHT Seen departing Paddington wearing revised Network SouthEast livery is No. 50003 *Temeraire*.

ABOVE LEFT
Contrasting liveries as Nos 50025 *Invincible* and 50046 *Ajax* are seen stabled at Old Oak Common.

ABOVE A lovely study of revised NSE-liveried No. 50003 *Temeraire* pauses with a matching rake of Mk1 stock.

LEFT Revised NSE-liveried No. 50024 *Vanguard* awaits a night-time departure from Reading.

LEFT No. 50017 *Royal Oak* readies for departure from Salisbury during the Class 50's swansong of regular booked services on the Waterloo–Exeter route.

RIGHT Lit by some bright spring sunshine, No. 50018 *Resolution* arrives at Gillingham with an Exeter-bound train on 30 March 1991.

LEFT No. 50027 *Lion* negotiates a single section of line on the Waterloo–Exeter route as it runs between Templecombe and Buckhorn Weston Tunnel on 5 August 1989.

By the summer of 1991 there was a final pool of 12 Class 50s appearing on Waterloo–Exeter trains. These were Nos D400 (50050 after being restored to its original identity), 50002 *Superb*, 50017 *Royal Oak*, 50018 *Resolution*, 50027 *Lion*, 50029 *Renown*, 50030 *Repulse*, 50031 *Hood*, 50033 *Glorious*, 50037 *Illustrious*, 50046 *Ajax* and 50049 *Defiance*.

Gradually, use of the Class 50s was run down, and the final day of their regular operation on the route came on 24 May 1992. On this day, which NSE held as a promotional event, Nos D400 and 50007 *Sir Edward Elgar* (the latter having just returned to traffic), hauled two double-headed return trips between Exeter and Salisbury. After 18 years on the route, the pair headed the last scheduled Class 50 revenue-earning, timetabled passenger service on BR with the 16.55 Waterloo–Exeter forward from Salisbury. On its front end No. 50007 carried a 'Farewell Class 50' headboard.

LEFT No. 50033 *Glorious* was affectionately known by Laira staff as 'old Smokey Joe', for reasons that are obvious from this view of it at Waterloo. However, because of this trait, the loco was banned from entering Waterloo station!

London Waterloo

Exeter Central – Whimple – Feniton – Honiton – **Axminster** – Crewkerne – **Yeovil Junction** – Sherborne – Templecombe – **Gillingham (Dorset)** – Tisbury – **Salisbury** – Andover – **Basingstoke** – **Woking**

Stations shown in red have short platforms.
Passengers are advised to travel in the correct portion of the train.

LEFT An original carriage label from an Exeter–London Waterloo service. Stations shown in red had short platforms and hence passengers were required to move to the correct portion of the train to alight at their destination.

ABOVE LEFT No. 50027 *Lion* speeds through Templecombe with an Exeter-bound service on 30 March 1991.

ABOVE The first Class 50 to be withdrawn was No. 50011 *Centurion*, which was taken out of service on 23 February 1987 and used as an engine test bed. It is seen here in better times at Old Oak Common.

LEFT No. 50033 *Glorious* emerges from the curve under Battledown flyover near Worting Junction. This loco had its nameplate positioned uniquely to read 'Glorious Network SouthEast'.

RIGHT The final day of regular Class 50 operation on the Waterloo–Exeter route came on 24 May 1992, which NSE held as a promotional event. Nos D400 and 50007 *Sir Edward Elgar* hauled two double-headed return trips. After 18 years on the route, the pair hauled the last scheduled Class 50 revenue-earning passenger service, the 16.55 Waterloo–Exeter. Green-liveried No. 50007 carried a 'Farewell Class 50' headboard, as seen in this view at Exeter.

37

ABOVE A line-up of six withdrawn Class 50s stored at Ocean Sidings, Plymouth.

RIGHT No. 50034 *Furious* was cut up by Coopers Metals at Old Oak Common on 12 May 1990.

BELOW No. 50024 *Vanguard* succumbed to the scrapman at Old Oak Common on 23 January 1991. It is seen here having been unceremoniously cut into two, but had had its number panel cut out. Many of these 'flame outs' were acquired by enthusiasts.

Fall and rise

Withdrawals of Class 50s had begun by the late 1980s, with No. 50011 *Centurion* being the first member of the class to go, on 24 February 1987. This loco was followed by No. 50006 *Neptune* on 20 July 1987. They were joined by several more classmates in the late 1980s, and during the early 1990s withdrawals rapidly gathered pace.

However, with the fate of the Class 50s sealed, some of the last members of the fleet to remain running with BR gained celebrity status. In 1984, No. 50007 *Hercules* had been repainted in GWR lined-green livery and was renamed *Sir Edward Elgar*. This loco went on to become a flagship of the Laira fleet and after

ABOVE Another view from the Old Oak Common Class 50 scrapline, as the partial remains of No. 50005 *Collingwood* await the loco's final fate.

LEFT Prior to the 'Midland Scotsman' railtour from Birmingham to Glasgow in February 1994, Geoff Hudson wanted another BR blue Class 50 to accompany No. D400 for the trip to Scotland. By this time, the BR Class 50 budget only covered routine maintenance and exams, so the repaint of No. 50033 as D433 was sponsored by Locomaster Profiles. Geoff arranged to have a set of sponsorship, lookalike leasing plaques fitted, and despite a heavy workload, the depot even managed to give No. D400 a fresh coat of blue paint. The two locos are pictured at Laira on 21 September 1994. There was a very smokey double fire-up! *(Paul Furtek)*

ABOVE The 'Midland Scotsman' railtour seen at Birmingham New Street on its return from Glasgow.

ABOVE One of the sponsorship plaques styled like the original English Electric leasing plates, fitted to No. D433 for the 'Midland Scotsman' railtour from Birmingham to Glasgow. Note misspelling of 'sponsored'! *(Paul Furtek)*

ABOVE An unusual working for No. 50033 *Glorious* occurred on 6 July 1992, following repairs to yet another traction motor generator, when it was sent on a test run from Laira to Bristol St Philips Marsh and back. This was a stock transfer move and the return to Laira – pictured at Taunton – saw No. 50033 towing HST power cars Nos 43022 and 43042. *(Paul Furtek)*

a restoration by apprentices at the depot went on to be a stalwart of the Class 50 run-down programme (see pages 32–33).

In January 1991, Nos 50008 *Thunderer* and 50015 *Valiant* received repaints in Departmental blue and Civil Engineers' 'Dutch' grey and yellow liveries respectively. These two gained a great following on railtour duties, and their last train as such took place on 23 November 1991, the 'Valiant Thunderer'. For this, No. 50015's nameplate background was painted black instead of red to give an authentic Civil Engineers' look. The pair were joined on the railtour by No. 50033 *Glorious*.

By early 1994, only three 50s remained running on the BR network – Nos D400, 50007 and 50033. In February, the clock was turned back a quarter of a century when D400 was joined in its all-over BR blue livery by 50033, which received a sponsored repaint as D433 by video production company Locomaster Profiles. The pair made the trip to Glasgow Central, where the last time Class 50s had been seen, more than 20 years previously, was a pair of blue-liveried D4xx-numbered locos.

For No. D433, this was a one-off appearance. The loco was to be presented to the National Railway Museum as part of

LEFT The unveiling of No. 50007 *Sir Edward Elgar* followed completion of its overhaul which had been rounded off with an immaculate repaint in lined GWR green. It had been withdrawn from traffic in 1990 with a main generator failure and the restoration work was undertaken by Laira's apprentices. *(Paul Furtek)*

the National Collection, and so was given a complete restoration both internally and externally, and repainted in the attractive and ubiquitous 1980s BR large-logo livery.

On 19 March 1994, a resplendent 50033 *Glorious* was joined by 50050 *Fearless*, also freshly repainted in large-logo blue livery, and 50007, for the 'Cornish Caper' railtour which, as well as reaching Penzance, visited branch lines taking the trio to Newquay, then later in the tour to St Ives.

The following day saw the 'Glorious Sunset' railtour run to York, where 50033 was to remain for its hand-over to the NRM, which took place on 1 April 1994.

The last BR Class 50-hauled train to run was the '50 Terminator' railtour on 23 March 1994, when 50050 *Fearless* and 50007 *Sir Edward Elgar* ran an outward leg from Waterloo to Penzance. The return journey was most appropriately from Penzance to Paddington, where the two 50s arrived with a wreath placed on *Fearless* and amid a fanfare of two-tone diesel horns! The Class 50's time with BR was over, as almost was BR's time itself.

However, even by this time the Class 50's popularity had meant that many had been bought for preservation. At one point, almost half the entire fleet had survived, as when the new millennium arrived no fewer than 23 still existed. However, after surviving the cutter's torch for some years, five of these were to succumb to being broken up as a result of their deteriorating condition. The number of preserved Class 50s, some 18, is still an impressive figure when considering the original size of the fleet.

When it is taken into account that numerous Class 50s have returned to the main line since The Fifty Fund led the way with No. 50031 *Hood* in 1997, just three years after the class was withdrawn from BR metals, it makes the class's subsequent history more a story of success, rather than just one of survival!

ABOVE Such was the immaculate restoration of No. 50033 for presentation to the National Railway Museum, that even the power unit was repainted! Geoff Hudson and some of Laira's staff stand proudly in front of the resplendent loco on 17 March 1994. (Paul Furtek)

BELOW Class pioneer No. 50050 *Fearless* waits at London Waterloo on 26 March 1994 prior to working the farewell '50 Terminator' railtour with No. 50007 *Sir Edward Elgar*. (Paul Furtek)

Former Laira fitter Mike Woodhouse describes the reason behind why No. 50049 became the choice to become the sole experimental Class 50/1, in this extract from his 1990 book of memoirs, *Blood, Sweat and Fifties*:

"1986 witnessed the rise of Network SouthEast and its distinctive red, white and blue livery. Most of the 50s were destined to end up in this garb, but some of the other newly formed sectors were also responsible for a share of the work performed by the class. With effect from the New Year of 1987 'it was rumoured' Railfreight would take over responsibility for ten locos. They were to form a sub-class, the 50/1, and be numbered 50101 to 50110. Arrangements were put in hand for the modification work to be done at BREL Doncaster Works. In the meantime no maintenance to the electric train heating equipment on the selected locos was to be allowed, and all operating expenses were to be charged to Railfreight.

"The locomotives chosen were 50001/003/005/010/012/015/022/024/050, with the tenth still to be decided. However, it quickly became apparent that the gang of nine were not dedicated to freight work, but used just the same as the rest of the class.

"In April 1987 Railfreight sector confirmed it would put up the money to modify the first unit. The selected loco would be one from the 'F' overhaul programme then underway at Laira, and all the work would be undertaken by the depot itself. In terms of modifications required, the 50/1 was to have re-geared Class 37 wheelsets and traction motors, a derating adjustment to the power unit, and disconnection of the ETH apparatus.

"So, which 50 would it be? 50050/028/044/049/043/005 was the provisional running order for the summer overhaul programme. As with all heavy maintenance to the 'Hoovers' I was actively involved, and played a part in each of the 23 'F' exams that Laira did. It was not until July that the re-geared bogies were delivered, and what with staff shortages plus 50050 (just starting its exam) requiring new bogies, it seemed that *Fearless* would become 50101 – or would it be 50150?

"However, it was not to be. After some delay '50 was given ordinary bogies and entered the Network SouthEast fleet; and so the honour fell to the next in line, which happened to be 50049 *Defiance*. Railfreight and the engineers from the Derby research HQ were pushing for a September release to traffic for trials, and so work began in earnest. '49 was berthed on No. 6 road stop blocks, and as well as the internal changes it was also to have the new Railfreight livery; Laira staff were to witness yet another new image. If the experiment was a success then this might be a

BELOW Experimental freight Class 50 No. 50149 *Defiance* on the Fowey branch at Golant with a rake of CDA china clay hoppers. *(Colour Rail)*

lifeline for some class members not down on the 'F' programme and thus facing early retirement.

"In early September 50049 finally gave way to 50149, repainted in three-tone grey with the distinctive red-and-yellow chequer of the Railfreight General sub-sector. A first for Laira was having its own depot badge cast – of a ship, what else! By the required date of 20 September all the finishing touches were complete and '149 was handed over to the Derby engineers. The Class 50/1 made its first trial run light engine to Totnes and back in the early afternoon of the 22nd.

"Its first real test came the next day on the afternoon shift. 47019, in charge of 6B43, the 14.25 St Blazey to Severn Tunnel Junction Speedlink freight, came light from Tavistock Junction Yard in order to collect *Defiance* for testing, while in the meantime the payload of the train had been made up to 960 tonnes. This proved almost too much for '149 and its derated 2,400hp power unit on the 1 in 42 of Hemerdon bank, as it very nearly stalled; but worse was to come.

"I was working on the next 'F' exam loco, 50043, when the call came through that '149 was off the road at Exeter. On being informed of the news I just could not believe it, but the foreman then came and told me and the rest of the breakdown gang to clear up what we were doing and make our way to the breakdown train. Our information was that 50149, 47019 and the leading wagon of the train had been derailed in Riverside Yard: a long shift was ahead.

"50029 *Renown* was provided to power the breakdown train, and good progress was made to Exeter. We pulled up alongside the derailment and got out to examine the damage. The two locos were going to be an easy lift as one bogie of each had just dropped off the road in a straight line. *Defiance* was the first to be re-railed, and once this was achieved I climbed aboard to restart the engine. As we waited for the air brake pressure to build the bogie was examined and the decision was taken to bring '149 home with us. '29 ran round and jumpered up to the 50/1, and then we recoupled the breakdown unit.

"Next came 47019, and as it was being re-railed the rest of 6B43 was shunted into an adjacent siding. By the time the loaded 75-tonne 'Tiger' clay wagon was back on the

LEFT Part of No. 50149's Railfreight General livery included Plymouth Laira depot plaques.

rails our job complete it was the early hours of the next morning, but at last we and the 50s could return to Laira.

"The official Railfreight launch was not until 15 October with adhesion trials planned the following weekend between Westbury and Warminster. Alas, disaster struck on the 8th, when '149 suffered a major engine failure at Yatton. 50014, working the Waterloo to Exeter route that day, was taken out of traffic to supply a replacement power unit (this being the last Fifty left with untreated mainframe fractures, 50006/011 already having been withdrawn). *Warspite* was later scrapped as a result. By working round the clock '149 was restored to health in time, but the trials were not a great success. No more 50/1s were authorised, and after 18 months *Defiance* was converted back to standard 50049 and returned to passenger work."

BELOW Royal Navy personnel from HMS *Defiance* following the rededication ceremony of No. 50149 at Laira on 18 August 1993. The loco had been purchased from BR by the Class 50 Society in December 1991. *(Paul Furtek)*

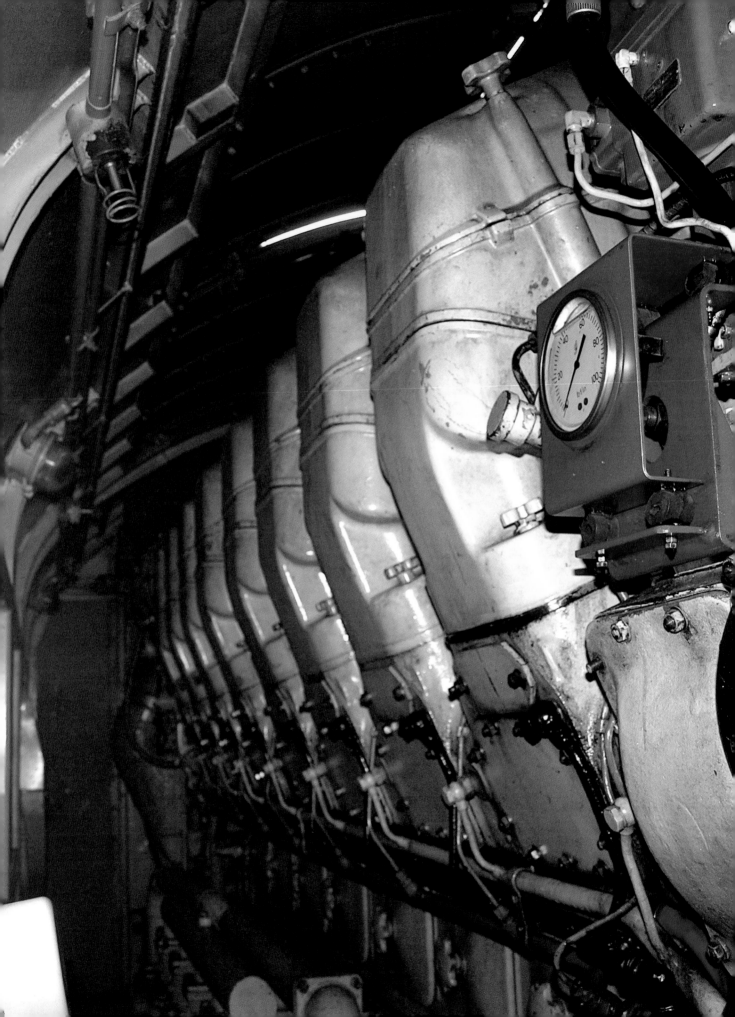

Chapter Two

Anatomy
of the
Class 50

When first delivered in 1967
the Class 50 was a revolution
in design with its complicated
electrical equipment. This
was especially so when it was
transferred to the Western Region
whose technicians were used to
diesel-hydraulics.

OPPOSITE Inside the engine room of No. 50035 *Ark Royal* with
the B bank of its EE 16CSVT power unit dominating the view.
The red gauge is a fuel-pressure gauge, fitted to this particular
locomotive as an experiment.

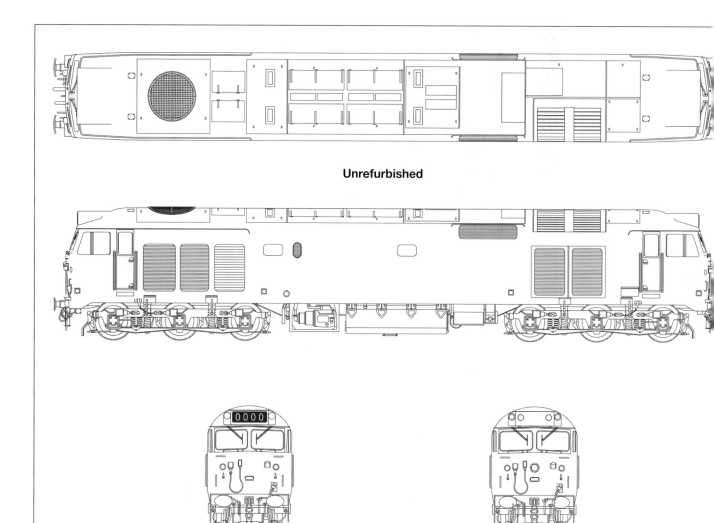

Unrefurbished

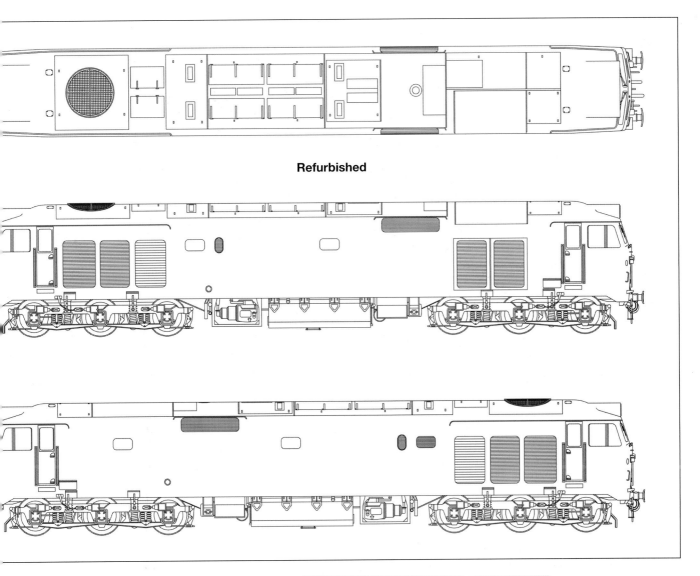

Refurbished

In this chapter the structure and some of the major systems of this ground-breaking diesel-electric locomotive are illustrated and described. The detailed colour photographs are of the inside of The Fifty Fund's No. 50035 *Ark Royal*, which is one of the most popular members of the fleet of locos surviving today.

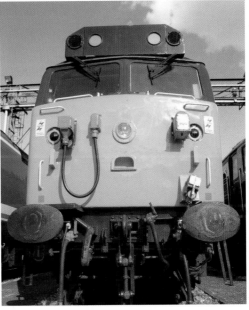

OPPOSITE The Fifty Fund's No. D444 was initially restored to refurbished condition with jumper cables and 'domino' marker lights, but was later given the full works, unrefurbished look with no jumper cables and operational headcode blinds. Viewed from No. 2 end, the cut-away section of the roof above the grilles can be seen.

ABOVE General arrangement drawings. *(Chris Sandham-Bailey/ Inkworm)*

LEFT For comparison with the view of No. D444, refurbished No. 50026 *Indomitable* is seen with the No. 1 end leading.

**Key to Class 50
front end layout
(refurbished)**

1 Multiple control
   jumper cable
2 Multiple control
   jumper receptacle
3 High intensity
   headlight
4 Tail lights
5 Electric train supply
   cable
6 Electric train supply
   socket
7 Main reservoir pipe
8 Vacuum pipe
9 Coupling equipment
10 Air brake pipe
11 Horns
12 Marker lights

General layout

EXTERNAL

The locomotive is carried on two, three-axle cast steel bogies. Between these bogies are mounted the compressors, air system reservoirs, main fuel tank and battery boxes. The battery isolating switch is accommodated in a cupboard at the end of the 'B' side battery box. The usual filling and draining facilities are provided at underframe level.

RIGHT **For comparison with the previous picture this is a close-up of the face of unrefurbished No. D444.**

BELOW **Early general arrangement drawings of a Class 50.** (British Rail)

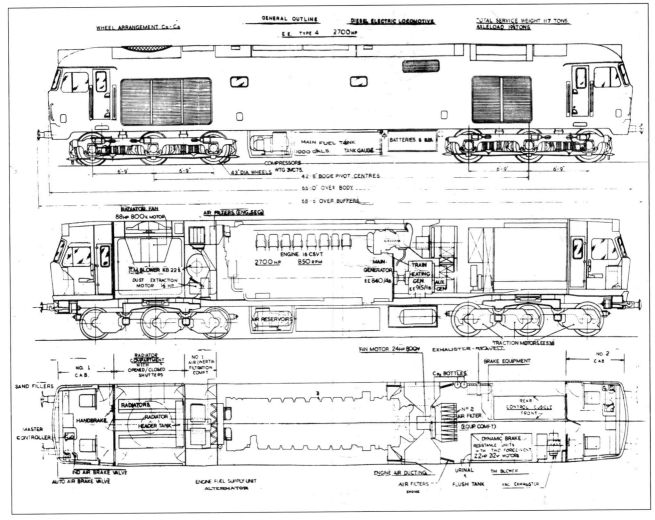

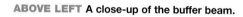

ABOVE LEFT A close-up of the buffer beam.

ABOVE Coupling and pipe attachment details.

LEFT Buffer and brake detail.

BELOW Multiple control jumper cable detail.

BELOW LEFT Multiple control jumper cable and receptacle, and ETH cable detail.

INTERNAL

The locomotive can be divided into five separate compartments:

- No. 1 cab
- Radiator compartment
- Clean air compartment
- Engine and control equipment compartment
- No. 2 cab

Cabs Nos 1 and 2

The cabs feature double-glazed side windows and thermostatically controlled air heating.

Air from the traction motor blower is heated as necessary by passing it through a heating box containing 2.8kw electric heating elements. A direction control handle to the right of the power controller enables the warm air to be directed to the driver's and secondman's feet as well as from a central position or from the central position only. The air flow cannot be shut off as this system provides for five to six changes of air in the cabs per hour.

Additional heat is provided by two convector type electric heaters in each cab. One cab is provided with a breakfast cooker and the other with a hot-plate.

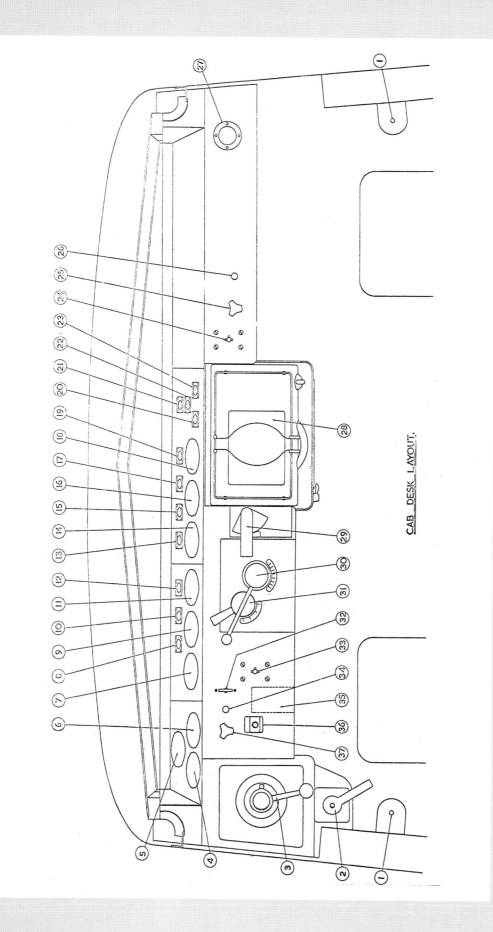

CAB DESK LAYOUT.

ABOVE The driver's position on No. 50035 *Ark Royal*.

1 Driver Safety Device (hand)
2 Straight air brake
3 Driver's automatic brake valve
4 Auto air brake
5 Duplex air gauge
6 Duplex vacuum gauge
7 Speedometer
8 Wheelslip light
9 Current setting control
10 Overload reset button
11 Main generator amps
12 Engine start button
13 Engine stop button
14 Slow speed indicator
15 General fault light
16 Slow speed control
17 Engine stop light
18 Main air pressure gauge
19 Fire alarm test
20 Train heating 'On' button
21 Train heating light
22 Dimmer switch
23 Train heating 'Off' button
24 Secondman's two-tone horn lever
25 Windscreen wiper control
26 Windscreen washer control
27 Vacuum relief valve
28 Cooker or hot-plate
29 Fan heater control
30 Power handle
31 Reverser handle
32 Dimmer switch, instrument lights
33 Driver's two-tone horn lever
34 Windscreen washer control
35 Driver Safety Device (foot)
36 Anti-slip button
37 Windscreen wiper control

ABOVE LEFT The secondman's position on No. 50035.

ABOVE Next to the master switch and power handle on No. 50031 is a cab-to-shore radio telephone.

FAR LEFT The AWS (automatic warning system) indicator and reset button on the driver's side of No. 50035.

LEFT A view of the rear of the No. 2 end cab of No. 50035.

LEFT Mounted at the rear of the cab are, to the left, seven fault lights and to the right, the AWS sounder and Baldwin valve.

RIGHT The battery isolating switch and main lighting circuit breaker box.

FAR RIGHT Battery isolating switch detail.

RIGHT Main lighting circuit breaker internal equipment.

BELOW No. 2 end traction motor blower.

Radiator compartment

The radiators are of the Spiral Tube pattern.

Pairs of panels are mounted, one behind the other, on either side of the locomotive. The outer panels are interconnected and cool the water circulating in the charge air coolers and the engine lubricating oil cooler. The two inner panels are also interconnected and cool the engine water jacket and turbo blower cooling water.

The radiator fan is driven by an 800-volt DC motor supplied from the train-heating generator output.

The fan has three speeds and a stop condition (only two locos – 007 and 043 –were originally had a stop condition) controlled by temperature-sensing devices. These devices also automatically control the operation of the radiator shutters which are opened and closed by compressed air.

Clean air compartment

This compartment contains the traction motor blower for No. 1 bogie, the suction-type inertia filters and inertia filter dust extraction fan, together with the engine air filters for the free end superchargers.

Engine and control equipment compartment

The engine is directly coupled to a main generator and by a shaft to the train heating and auxiliary generators. A pressurising fan mounted in ducting above the train heating generator forces air through another inertia filter system, pressurising the compartment with filtered air.

LEFT A brand-new EE 16CSTV power unit prior to installation in 1967. *(English Electric)*

This filtered air passes through a set of secondary filters which are mounted on ducting connected to the driving and turbochargers.

Adjacent to the auxiliary generator on 'A' bank side are two CO_2 fire extinguisher bottles, an exhauster, brake equipment cubicle and the main electrical control cubicle.

On 'B' bank side there is a urinal, two rheostatic brake resistor cubicles, an exhauster and a traction motor blower for No. 2 bogie.

The diesel engine installed in these locomotives is the English Electric 16-cylinder Vee-Type; pressure charged with intercooling.

Intercoolers or charge air coolers are small radiators situated between the turbochargers and the air manifold to the cylinders of the

LEFT The view down the 'thin man's side' with the control cubicle doors all closed.

BELOW LEFT The view down B bank, looking in from No. 2 end, over the main generator (with the orange terminal box), and under the turbocharger, past the governor.

BELOW Engine gauges on the power unit of No. 50035.

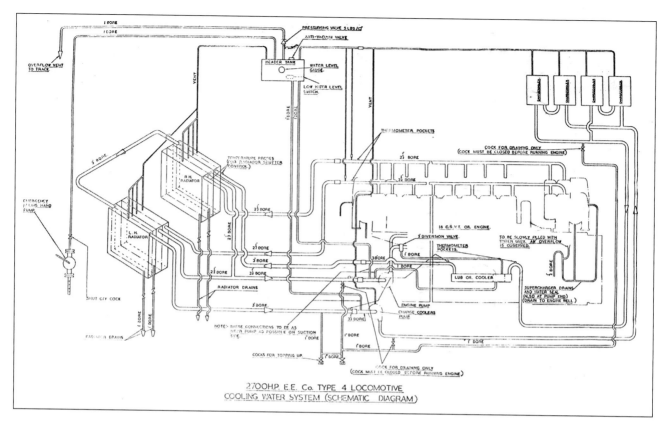

2700H.P. E.E. Co. TYPE 4 LOCOMOTIVE
COOLING WATER SYSTEM (SCHEMATIC DIAGRAM)

ABOVE A schematic diagram of the cooling water system.
(British Rail)

diesel engine. These radiators cool the air which has been compressed in the turbochargers, increasing its density and allowing more fuel to be burnt in the cylinders.

The engine speed range is 450–850rpm and the rating is 2,700hp.

The cooling water system

There are two cooling water systems, both being topped up from a common header tank, which is provided with two dial-type level gauges and a low-water protection switch.

The header tank gauges are located in the radiator compartment gangways in the rear of the radiators and adjacent to the clean air compartment bulkhead.

RIGHT
A turbocharger.

All the cooling water, with the exception of the header tank, is in circulation when the engine is running. Both systems are monitored for temperature variations by temperature-sensing devices which control the radiator shutters and radiator fan speeds.

There are two engine-driven water pumps located at the free end of the engine. The water from the pump on 'A' bank divides and circulates under pressure through the cylinder block, cylinder heads and turbochargers on each bank of cylinders; from there to the inner double banks of radiator elements. After passing through the radiators, it combines in a common return feed pipe to the suction side of the pump.

The water from 'B' bank pump circulates under pressure through the four intercoolers then to the heat exchanger and to the outer banks of radiator elements, before returning to the suction side of the pump.

Under very cold conditions, up to 80°F water temperatures, an electrically controlled diversion valve allows water to pass through a small section of the heat exchanger in order to raise the temperature of the intercoolers, and therefore the air passing through them.

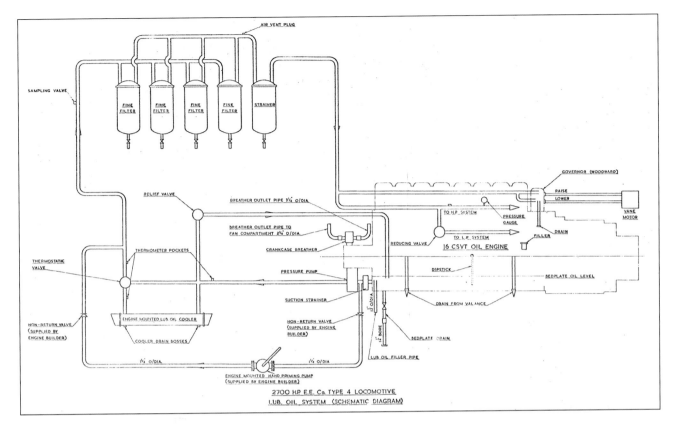

Labels in diagram:
AIR VENT PLUG
SAMPLING VALVE
FINE FILTER / FINE FILTER / FINE FILTER / FINE FILTER / STRAINER
GOVERNOR (WOODWARD)
RAISE / LOWER
RELIEF VALVE
BREATHER OUTLET PIPE 3¼ O/DIA
VANE MOTOR
BREATHER OUTLET PIPE TO FAN COMPARTMENT 2¼ O/DIA
TO H.P. SYSTEM
PRESSURE GAUGE
CRANKCASE BREATHER
REDUCING VALVE
TO L.P. SYSTEM
16 CSVT OIL ENGINE
FILLER
DRAIN
THERMOSTATIC VALVE
THERMOMETER POCKETS
PRESSURE PUMP
DIPSTICK
BEDPLATE OIL LEVEL
SUCTION STRAINER
NON-RETURN VALVE (SUPPLIED BY ENGINE BUILDER)
ENGINE MOUNTED LUB OIL COOLER
COOLER DRAIN BOSSES
NON-RETURN VALVE (SUPPLIED BY ENGINE BUILDER)
DRAIN FROM VALANCE
BEDPLATE DRAIN
LUB OIL FILLER PIPE
1¼ O/DIA
1¼ O/DIA
ENGINE MOUNTED HAND PRIMING PUMP (SUPPLIED BY ENGINE BUILDER)
2700 HP E.E. Co TYPE 4 LOCOMOTIVE LUB. OIL SYSTEM (SCHEMATIC DIAGRAM)

This is necessary as prolonged high cylinder pressures are undesirable, which would be the case if the air delivered to the cylinders remained cold.

Engine coolant temperature

At 160°F	Shutters open and low fan speed
At 170°F	Intermediate fan speed
At 180°F	Top fan speed
At 200°F	Fault light bright

Inertia air filtration

The clean air required for the engine and auxiliary equipment on this locomotive is drawn through louvres in the bodyside and passed through inertia-type filters.

The inertia filter works on the principle that if the direction of flow of dust-laden air is suddenly reversed, inertia causes the dust to continue travelling in the original direction of flow and thus become separated from the main air stream. About 10% of the air which enters the filter is carried off with the dust into ducting at the rear of the element.

At the drive-end of the engine compartment, and mounted above the train heating and auxiliary generators, is a pressurising fan and two banks of inertia filter elements. This fan forces air through the elements and the 10% air bleed with the extracted dust is automatically blown down through ducting to the track.

Adjacent to the free end of the engine is a clean air compartment which is subjected to a partial vacuum created by the action of the turbochargers, and No. 1 traction motor blower. The air is drawn into this compartment through the inertia filters mounted near the roof on each side of the compartment. In this case, the 10% air bleed and extracted dirt from these filters is drawn off by a small dust extraction fan, which also exhausts downwards on to the track.

Lubricating oil system

Lubricating oil is drawn from the sump (capacity 120gal) through a suction strainer by an engine-driven lubricating oil sump. The oil pressure on the delivery side of the pump is set to $70lb/in^2$ by a relief valve. Oil at this pressure then flows to a thermostatic valve which bypasses the oil cooler initially allowing the oil to flow to four fine filters and one strainer before delivery to the engine high-pressure system, feeding the bearings in the usual manner.

ABOVE A schematic diagram of the lubricating oil system. *(British Rail)*

RIGHT Oil and water drains.

FAR RIGHT An English Electric builder's plate as fitted to No. D444.

FAR RIGHT Sandbox filler detail.

RIGHT High-intensity headlight detail.

FAR RIGHT Orange square coupling restriction marking.

BELOW A high view of No. 50014 *Warspite* from the wall at Penzance reveals the roof detail of a Class 50.

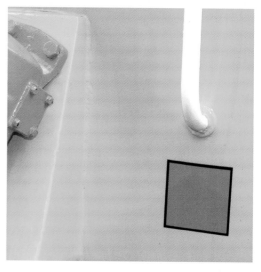

When the oil temperature reaches 149ºF the thermostatic valve allows the oil to flow through the oil cooler.

NOTE: If the thermostatic valve fails to operate, provision is made for manual operation by screwing down on top of the valve with the ring spanner provided.

A hand-priming pump is fitted on the 'B' bank side of the engine bedplate, and should be operated before starting if the engine is cold.

A lubricating oil filter is located adjacent to this pump and the usual connections for filling the sump are provided outside the locomotive at solebar level.

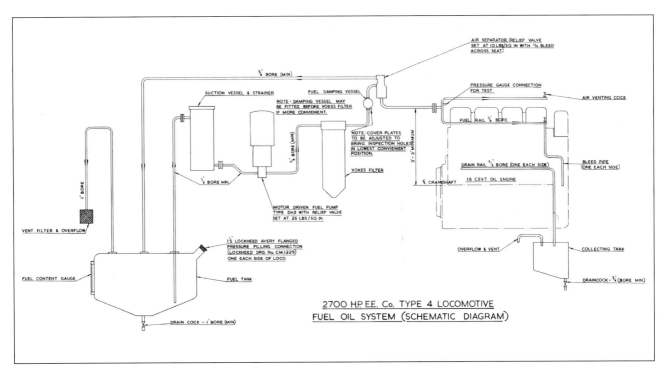

The dipstick is located on 'A' bank side and is graduated as follows:

- Maximum standing
- Maximum running
- Minimum standing

A further reducing valve is fitted in the engine high-pressure system set at $2\frac{1}{2}$lb/in^2, providing low pressure oil for lubricating the rocker gear etc.

Fuel oil system

The locomotive is fitted with a 1,100gal fuel tank, which incorporates a sight glass contents gauge at each side, together with a low-level warning float switch (set to operate at approximately 200gal). Flight refuelling valves avoid the over-filling of the tank.

Fuel is drawn from this tank by an electrically driven transfer pump (with a relief valve set at 25lb/in^2), through a combined suction vessel and strainer, to a Vokes fine filter. The fuel then passes through a damping vessel to the air separator with a relief valve set at 10lb/in^2 and 1/16in air bleed hole across the seat. From the air separator the fuel is delivered to the bus rails and injection pumps in the usual way.

Fuel in excess of engine requirements returns from the 10lb/in^2 relief valve direct to the fuel tank.

Air and vacuum systems

The following is a description of the function of the equipment provided on the locomotive for braking, control etc. The actual position on the locomotive of the various valves is also mentioned

LEFT Fuel tank filler and sight gauge.

ABOVE Fuel tank detail.

RIGHT The oil priming pump, which is manually operated to get up a good sweat before you start the loco!

where appropriate. The majority (but not all) of the Westinghouse fittings are grouped together, behind the auxiliary generator and in front of the control cubicle. This will be referred to as the 'Westinghouse frame' and the position of any component on this will be described as seen when standing facing the frame with one's back to the auxiliary generator, and facing No. 2 cab.

Main air supply

Two Westinghouse compressors mounted underframe on the left and right sides ahead of the fuel tank draw air piped from the engine room. An air strainer and anti-freezer serves each compressor, which are on each side of the engine. The compressed air is stored in four main reservoirs (two ahead of the fuel tank between the compressors, and two to the rear of the fuel tank, between the battery boxes).

A pressure switch, fitted with an isolating cock (in the engine room, on 'A Bank' side close to the auxiliary generator) acts as a compressor governor, cutting in and out the compressor motor contacts to maintain a pressure of 118–140lb/in^2. A safety valve is

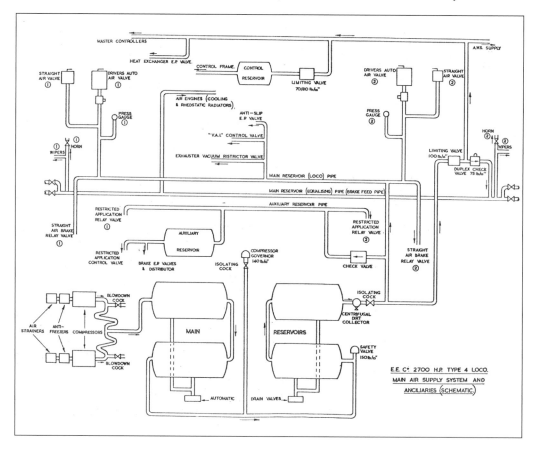

RIGHT A schematic diagram of the main air supply and ancillaries. (British Rail)

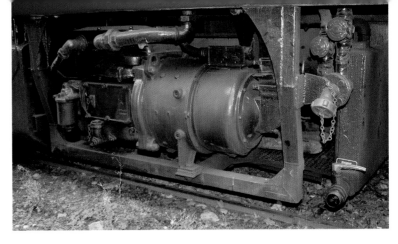

fitted close to the right-hand rear reservoir, which is set to lift at 150lb/in^2. The supply from the reservoirs is taken through a centrifugal dirt collector and isolating cock (close to the left-hand rear reservoir) and has three functions:

- Directly supplies the driver's brake valves, pressure gauges, straight air brake relay valve, anti-slip EP valve and air-operated components in the vacuum system.
- Supplies the auxiliary reservoir through a check valve (alongside left-hand rear main reservoir). The auxiliary reservoir is situated between the fuel tank and the two rear main reservoirs and supplies those components which it is important should have air available in an emergency: e.g. automatic brake control and relay valves, the distributor and brake EP valves. The check valve ensures the air in the auxiliary reservoir cannot be lost back into the main reservoir system in the event of a breakdown, pipe fracture or compressor failure.
- Supplies, via a 100lb/in^2 limiting valve, the AWS system and the master controllers. The 100lb/in^2 supply also feeds the main reservoir

equalising pipe (or brake feed pipe) which can be coupled up to an adjacent locomotive or to an air-braked train working on the 'two-pipe' system. A duplex check valve ensures that if the air on the locomotive is being used to keep another 'dead' locomotive supplied, or there is undue leakage in the brake feed pipe on the train, the air pressure in the main system of the supplying locomotive cannot fall below
75lb/in^2. The main reservoir equalising pipe (or brake feed pipe) is fitted with ¾in flexible connections beside the buffers on each end of the locomotive, and also supplies the horns, windscreen wipers and washers.

ABOVE Air compressor detail.

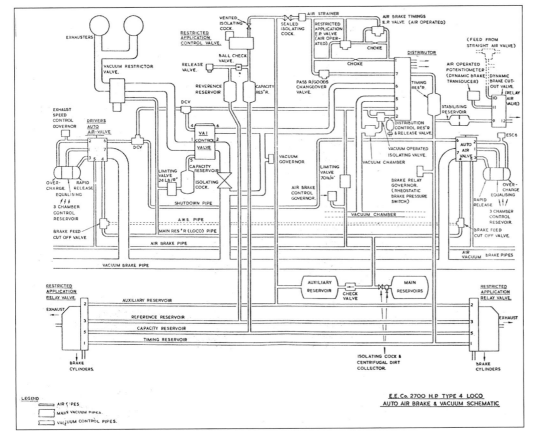

LEFT A schematic diagram of the automatic air-brake and vacuum system.
(British Rail)

ABOVE The brake frame, pneumatic control and distribution of the air and vacuum.

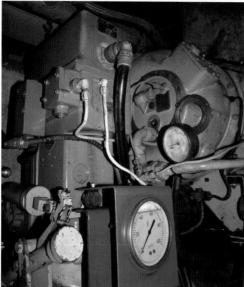

RIGHT The diesel set governor which regulates the speed of the diesel engine to compensate for changes in load.

FOUR-POSITION TRAIN IDENTIFICATION SYSTEM

When built, the Class 50s featured a headcode box fitted with the four-position numbers/letters blind equipment as was used at that time. The system of displaying the train headcode on the front of the loco was abandoned from 1 January 1976, and so this equipment became redundant. On most locomotives the headcode blinds were wound to 0000. Later, towards the end of 1976, most Class 50s had their blinds wound to display their class, followed by the relative locomotive's number. Of course, as this comprised five digits the display had to miss out the central '0', hence No. 50001 displayed 5001 in its headcode box. This lasted until the blinds were replaced with black panels containing two round white marker lights.

The following is a description of how the system worked, as issued in 1961 to BR staff working on the LMR.

General

A new system of classifying and identifying trains by means of a four-position description was introduced with the Summer Working Timetables commencing 12 June 1961, as follows:

Passenger trains

■ All Class A trains.
■ All Class C (parcels) trains.
■ Class B trains and Class C (empty coaching stock) trains running over sections of the line where modern train describers are used for train signalling, or where trains equipped with four-position indicators operate.

Freight trains

All classes of freight trains running over sections of the line where modern train describers are used for train signalling, or where locomotives equipped with four-position indicators operate.

This system introduces a new method

of indicating all movements on running lines between signal boxes, by use of a four-position number, incorporating the headcode, the destination district, and a distinctive identity number.

It will be applied as follows and gradually extended to cover ALL trains.

- Allocation of numbers to all trains in Working Timetables, Special Traffic Notices, Special Notices and other relevant operating publications.
- Exhibition of numbers on locomotives and multiple unit trains, which have been equipped with four-position indicator boxes, superseding the existing headcode instructions. Electric and diesel locomotives and multiple units fitted with four-positions indicator boxes are now being delivered. In future, all such new power will be so equipped and the fitting of indicator equipment to earlier diesel locomotives and multiple units will take place as they pass through the works.
- Transmission of numbers between signal boxes in modern train describer signalling installations. By means of this equipment train descriptions can be set up on the panel by the signalmen at any point and will then be transmitted automatically from one signal box to the next.

It is anticipated that by Summer 1962, all trains will have been allocated four-position numbers. The extent to which the new system can be used in full will vary in different parts of the Region until electrification, dieselisation and signalling re-equipment programmes are completed.

Basis of the scheme
A standard code has been devised providing for the identification of class, destination and number of all trains.

Main line passenger and freight trains are allocated individual numbers which are not duplicated over any one section of line. Local passenger and empty coaching stock trains are allocated route numbers, and freight trip trains are allocated trip numbers,

ABOVE The displaying of train headcode numbers on locos was abandoned by BR from 1 January 1976. On most locomotives, the headcode blinds were wound to 0000 until they were replaced with black panels containing round white marker lights. Here, two Class 50s and a Class 52 'Western' stand at Paddington, all three locomotives displaying 0000. It is well known that Class 50s gained the nickname 'Hoovers' because of the noise made by their clean air plant at the No. 2 end, prior to refurbishment, which was likened to that of a vacuum cleaner. However, what some may not realise is that is it believed the name was first given to them by the station staff at Paddington.

LEFT A poor quality but rare colour photo showing No. 50039 *Implacable* at Paddington with the 1B55 departure to Paignton, on 30 December 1974. In the background is an unidentified 50 with the 1B60 departure to Cardiff.

LEFT No. 50045 stands at Plymouth with all noughts wound in its headcode box following the abandonment of their use.

which in view of the number of trains involved are more suitable to local working.

First position	Class of Train (existing headcode)	Numbers 0 to 9
Second position	Destination	Letters of the alphabet (excluding I, Q, R, U, W and Y)
Third and fourth positions	Individual train numbers*	Numbers 0 to 9

*Local passenger and empty coaching stock trains are indicated by a ROUTE number.

Freight trips are indicated by a TRIP number.

Explanation of the system

The train numbers are based on the following code:

First position indicates Classification of train.
No.
1 - Class A train
2 - Class B train
3 - Class C parcels etc. train
    Class C ecs train
4 - Class C freight train
5 - Class D freight train
6 - Class E freight train
7 - Class F freight train
8 - Class H freight train
9 - Class J freight train
0 - Light engine(s). Engine and brake van

Notes

The full Classification indication is detailed in the Supplementary Operating Instructions, dated October 1960.

Class K freight trains are redesignated Class J.

Light engines to work all trains, carrying the number 0 in the first position, are allocated the destination letter and identity numbers of the train worked in the second, third and fourth positions.

Light engines, local to the London Midland Region NOT to work a train (e.g. to shunt) or running to a motive power depot are numbered 0Z00. Similar inter-regional light engines are allocated the second position letter of the destination region (e.g. Light engine to Western Region depot 0V00).

Second position indicates the Destination District of the train

The second position identifies the destination district for trains local to the London Midland Region, or destination region for inter-regional trains. The District Operating/Traffic Superintendents' districts have been used as the destination districts and some grouping has been necessary.

In view of the large number of express trains into the Preston District on Saturdays in the summer, the Blackpool and Fylde area has been allocated a separate letter.

The Euston and Manchester North Districts have been allocated two letters to allow sufficient numbers for the Saturday-only express trains.

Trains running within the London Midland Region

Letter	Destination District
A	Euston
B	Euston
	Rugby
C	St. Pancras
	Marylebone
	Manchester North
D	Chester
	Nottingham
F	Leicester
G	Birmingham
H	Manchester South
	Stoke-on-Trent
J	Manchester North
K	Crewe
	Liverpool Lime Street
	Liverpool Central
L	Preston (excluding Fylde)
	Barrow
	Carlisle
P	Blackpool and Fylde
	Derby

Inter-Regional trains

Letter	Destination region
E	Eastern
M	London Midland
N	North Eastern
O	Southern
S	Scottish
V	Western

NOTES

Excursion and special passenger and special freight trains are indicated as follows:

T	Passenger	Local to LMR
Z	Passenger and freight	
X	Passenger and freight	Inter-Regional

For freight trains T indicates trip train.

Third and fourth positions indicate Identity Number of train

Express passenger and freight trains (excluding trips) are allocated individual identity numbers to each district, between 00 and 99.

e.g. Through freight train to Chaddesden – 8P46

Parcels etc. trains are allocated individual identity numbers to each district between 00 and 29. e.g. Parcels train to Oldham – 3J14

Inter-district empty coaching stock trains NOT to work a train (e.g. trains required to transfer stock between districts for balancing purposes, or in connection with excursion or special traffic) are allocated individual identity numbers to each district, between 30 and 49.

e.g. Special empty coaching stock train Barrow to Willesden – 3Z46

Class B and local empty coaching stock trains are allocated route numbers in each district between 50 and 99. The route numbers relate to the local pattern of services and apply in both directions of travel. They are included in the appropriate sections of the Working Timetables. For inter-district and inter-regional trains common route numbers are allocated although the second position letter is altered according to the destination district or region of the train.

e.g. Local train
Manchester Ex. to Huddersfield – 2N96}
Huddersfield to Manchester Ex. – 2M96}
Freight trips are allocated trip numbers in each district between 00 and 99

e.g. Mineral trip No. 82 – 9T82

Existing trips will be suitably renumbered to conform with this arrangement.

BELOW As an interim measure, only No. 50003, as seen here, and No. 50035 were fitted with this style of bulbous marker lights.

Chapter Three

The driver's view

The Class 50s were to become very popular with their drivers, some of whom even became keen enthusiasts of these Type 4s!

OPPOSITE Exeter driver John Morton at the controls of No. 50007 *Sir Edward Elgar* while climbing the South Devon banks on the outward leg of the '50 Terminator' railtour. *(Paul Furtek)*

The following is taken from the *Preliminary Driving Instructions* for the class, as issued by English Electric in November 1967.

English Electric Co Ltd

2,700hp Diesel-Electric Locomotives Nos D400–D449

The first part of these instructions deals with drivers' daily duties, preparation and disposal duties, train working and operation of the locomotive in traffic.

This is followed by a section dealing with fuses and miniature circuit breakers and fault-finding charts.

Daily duties

- Obtain master, carriage and door keys.
- Test fire alarm warning system by pressing a test button.
- Check that the detonator cases are intact.
- Report all known defects.

Introduction to preparation duties

Reference to the diagram 'Preparation of Locomotive' will assist the driver by indicating the 'route' he should take (when preparing the locomotive) for either No. 1 cab or No. 2 cab leading, to ensure all essential features are covered. The diagram also shows the position of various cocks, gauges and switches etc. which will help the driver during his preparation and subsequent working of the locomotive.

BELOW The driver of No. 50031 *Hood* awaits departure from Plymouth.

Preparation duties – No. 1 cab leading

At locomotive

- Leave cab by 'B' side door.
- Ensure that no depot pipe or electric cables are attached.
- Check the air and vacuum pipes are secure on their plugs at No. 1 end of locomotive and ensure the air cocks are closed and in addition, check the jumper cables (including train heating) are secure in their respective sockets.
- Proceed along 'A' side of locomotive.
- Check main fuel contents gauge. (Sight glass on side of tank.)
- Check air and vacuum pipes are secure on plugs at No. 2 end of locomotive, check the air pipe cocks are closed and, in addition, check the jumper cables (including train heating) are secure in their respective sockets. Return to driving cab along the other side of the unit.
- Turn battery isolating switch to the 'On' position. This is on the battery control box towards No. 2 end of the locomotive on 'B' bank, outside.
- This will enable lights to be turned on, but these will go out after 15 minutes unless the engine has been started.

In driving cab No. 1 end

- Check the handbrake is 'On'.
- Check the air brake handle is in the 'Release' position and the auto air brake valve is in the 'Shutdown' position.
- Take the master key and carriage key.
- Proceed to the clean air compartment through 'A' side of locomotive.
- Check the safety pins are removed from the main fire extinguishers in the clean air compartment, and return to the cab. See the engine and clean air compartment doors are closed behind you.
- Proceed to the non-driving cab through the engine room; along 'B' side.
- Check radiator water in header tank and check the engine and clean air compartment doors are closed.
  NOTE: The radiator shutters on this locomotive are automatically controlled and require no adjustment.

- Operate hand priming lubricating oil pump on engine for 30 double strokes if the engine is cold.
- Check the safety pins are removed from the main fire extinguishers opposite the auxiliary generator; if not, remove them.
- Check the traction motor switches are in the 'Normal' position.
- Circuit breakers are in the 'On' position and spare fuses in position.
- Compressor switch in the 'Normal' position.
- Air/Vacuum switch is in the 'Air/Goods' position.

In non-driving cab (No. 2 end)
- Insert the master key and unlock controller, then move the reversing handle to the 'EO' position.
- Check the auto air brake valve handle is in the 'Shutdown' position and the straight air brake valve handle is in the 'Release' position.
- Check the AWS change-end switch is in the 'Off' position.
- Press engine start button. (See note on starting engine.)
- Check the detonator case is intact and the hand extinguisher is in position.
- Operate fire alarm test button on the desk.
- Set route indicators to blank aspect if necessary.
- Check the doors and windows are closed.
   - Check all vacuum is released from the chamber side, operating the vacuum release valve if necessary. Allow main reservoir pressure to rise to at least 100psi.
   - Move the driver's automatic air brake handle from the 'Shutdown' to the 'Running' position and immediately air pressure of 70psi should be obtained on the auto air brake pipe gauge. Allow approximately one minute for the distributor air chamber to charge, then move the handle to the distributor air chamber to charge then move the handle to the 'First application' position and then towards the 'Full service' position and check the auto air brake pipe pressure falls, and the brake cylinder pressure rises at a controlled rate consistent with the operation of air-braked freight trains.

- At the 'Full service' position the auto air brake pipe pressure should be approximately 48psi and the brake cylinder pressures approximately 85psi. Then move the handle to 'Emergency' position and note that when the auto air brake pipe pressure falls to zero the brake cylinder pressures remain at approximately 85psi. Now move the automatic brake valve handle to 'Shutdown' position. The power brake will remain on.
   - Place the reversing handle to 'Off', then remove the master key, leaving the engine running, then release the handbrake.
- Proceed to the driving cab through the engine room.
- En route, place the Air/Vacuum switch to 'Vacuum passenger'. Also make a cursory

ABOVE A Class 50 train crew and station staff have a discussion at Plymouth.

BELOW No. 50047 waits at Preston with 1S76. *(Tony Wright)*

ABOVE The driver of No. 50018 *Resolution* cleans the loco's windscreen.

BELOW The driver of original Network SouthEast-liveried No. 50023 *Howe* powers his charge on a westbound service.

- Operate the fire alarm test button.
- Reset route indicators if necessary.
- Check the detonator case is intact and the hand fire extinguisher is in position.
- To test the brakes with the above pressure available:
  - ♦ Move the straight air brake valve handle towards the 'Full service' position, checking the brake cylinder pressures rise; return straight air brake handle to 'Release' position.
  - ♦ Move the automatic air brake handle into 'First application' position and then towards the 'Full service' position; note that the auto air brake pipe pressure falls, the vacuum train pipe vacuum falls, and the air brake cylinder pressures rise. NOTE: With the automatic air brake handle in the 'Full service' position the auto air brake pipe pressure should be approximately 48psi, the train pipe vacuum falls to zero, and the brake cylinder pressures rise to approximately 85psi.
  - ♦ Move the auto air brake valve handle to 'Emergency' position and note the auto air brake pipe pressure falls rapidly to zero.
  - ♦ Return the auto air brake valve handle to the 'Running' position and check the auto air brake pipe pressure is restored to 70psi and that the vacuum train pipe gauge and the air brake cylinders gauges indicate the normal running values of 21in and zero, respectively.
  - ♦ Move the reversing handle to the 'Forward' position, release the handbrake and at the same time, check the driver's safety device operates.

NOTES:
- ♦ The auto air brake valve is the self-lapping type. A release position is provided on this valve for use when working air-braked and vacuum-fitted trains to enable the brake pipe to be recharged or the vacuum brake to be released quickly.
- ♦ The AWS change-end switch is provided with a fixed handle on this locomotive.

Sound the warning horns

When sounding the horns to comply with Rule 127 and the appendix instruction,

examination of the engine and generator compartments for any obvious defects and check the other side doors are secure, close engine room bulkhead doors and enter the driving cab.

- Insert the master key and unlock the controller then move the reversing handle to the 'EO' position. The exhausters and one compressor will now start (the second compressor is not in use with the Air/Vacuum switch in a 'Vacuum' position). Move the AWS key to 'On' then depress and release the AWS reset button.
- Move the auto air brake valve handle from the 'Shutdown' position to the 'Running' position. Check there is 118–140lb pressure on the main reservoir gauge and that the automatic air brake pipe pressure indicated on the cab gauge is 70psi and 21in vacuum is recorded on the vacuum gauge.

operate the lever in such a manner as to give the two-note sounds that these horns are designed to emit. This is of the utmost importance and if the horn is defective it must be reported immediately. (Horn tones were: High – E; Low – G.)

Starting the engine

■ If the engine is cold, operate the hand-priming lubricating oil pump on the engine for 30 double strokes. If the engine is warm, it is not necessary to operate this pump.

■ Place the master key in the controller and turn to the unlocked position.

■ Place the reversing handle into 'EO' position.

■ Press the engine start button firmly and hold it there until the engine fires and the 'Engine Stopped' red light goes dim. A local 'Start' button is provided in the engine room and can be used if desired as an alternative. The reversing handle must be in the 'EO' position in the driving cab before this 'Start' button will operate.

■ When the engine is started, No. 1 compressor starts immediately, but a time-delay device delays the start of No. 2 compressor for approximately five seconds. (The compressors work alternately, i.e. No. 1 compressor runs when driving from No. 1 cab in 'Forward' and No. 2 compressor runs when driving from No. 2 cab in 'Forward' with the air/vacuum switch in a 'Vacuum' position.)

NOTES:

◆ Under no circumstances must the 'Start' button be kept depressed if the engine fails to turn over within 10 seconds. If the engine runs but does not fire after approximately 15 seconds check that the governor shutdown button is 'In'. If no cause is apparent to the driver, the matter must be reported.

If low lubricating oil shutdown occurs, the button may be pushed in and the engine restarted. If the lubricating oil pressure is not established at idling speed, a time-delay action in the shutdown device in the governor will operate and again, shut down the engine in about 10 seconds.

◆ With the engine running and the reverser handle in the 'EO' position no power circuits are made, but the auxiliary generator provides power for the auxiliary machines and battery charging. The train heating generator provides power for the radiator fan and the pressurising fan

ABOVE No. 50010 *Monarch* climbs Dainton bank with a Paddington–Penzance train on 7 September 1985.

BELOW No. 50035 *Ark Royal* charges towards the camera in November 1988.

RIGHT An unidentified
Class 50 storms along
the Devon sea wall
during the late 1980s.

motors, and will provide approximately
⅔ full train-heating output at engine idling
speed.

To start the locomotive

Before attempting to move the locomotive
make sure the main reservoir air pressure is at
least 118psi and that 21in of vacuum is being
maintained by the exhausters.

Place the 'Air/Vacuum' switch in the
appropriate position. When running light
locomotive, or when hauling passenger trains
(including Freightliner trains), the switch MUST

be placed in the appropriate 'Passenger'
position. When hauling goods trains, including
those which are fully fitted the switch MUST be
placed in the appropriate 'Goods' position.

NOTE: When the 'Air/Vacuum' switch is
placed into the 'Goods' position the restricted
rate of brake build-up of 25 seconds will apply
not only to AWS, 'Driver's Safety Device' (DSD)
and guard applications, for severance of the
vacuum/air brake pipe, but to all driver-initiated
applications of the automatic air-brake valve.

Move AWS switch to 'On', then depress and
release the AWS reset button.

Release the handbrake.

Place a foot on the 'Driver's Safety Device'
pedal and depress it, then move the reversing
handle into 'Forward' or 'Reverse' for the
desired direction of travel.

NOTE: The AWS and DSD are air-controlled
on this locomotive. The DSD pedal has three
positions:

■ Released position
■ Balanced or 'mid' position
■ Depressed or 'reset' position.

A vigilance timing device will operate an audible
warning after the pedal has been held in the
balanced position for one minute. The pedal

BELOW No. 50002
Superb heads the
11.15 Waterloo–Exeter
out of Andover on 27
July 1991.

must be fully depressed and returned to the 'mid' or 'balanced' position to cancel and 'reset'. (Failure to do this will mean a brake application within five to seven seconds.) If during the one-minute cycle the AWS is reset, the DSD will automatically reset. However, resetting the DSD will not cancel the AWS.

If the pedal is released or depressed, the audible warning sounds immediately and five to seven seconds later, the brakes are applied in the normal manner. Three-position hold-over buttons are situated on the driver's and the secondman's sides of the cab and operate in the same manner as the pedal.

To move the locomotive

Release the holding air brake application, pull the power handle slowly away from the 'Off' position until the main ammeter registers a reading, then advance the handle gradually until the power required is obtained.

Care should be taken during acceleration not to allow the current to exceed 2,500 amps.

Current between 2,000 and 2,500 amps may be used for brief periods to start a train, but under these conditions the locomotive must move within three seconds, and under motion, should not be used for more than two or three minutes.

Currents up to 1,800 amps may be used continuously.

NOTE: When starting on a rising gradient, the air brake should be released as the main power handle is advanced. If the locomotive starts to run back when the brakes are released, reapply the brakes and return the main power handle to 'Off' before making a second attempt to move off. ON NO ACCOUNT MUST POWER BE APPLIED TO THE LOCOMOTIVE WHILST IT IS MOVING IN THE OPPOSITE DIRECTION TO THAT FOR WHICH THE REVERSER HANDLE IS SET.

Current limit setting

These locomotives were originally fitted with a current limit setting control which enables the driver to select any current between 0 and 'Max'. This is particularly useful under difficult starting conditions.

The current limit setting control on the desk is calibrated ¼, ½, ¾ and 'Max'. These positions indicate approximately 600, 1,200,

1,800 and 'Max' amps. The control equipment will automatically maintain the selected value during the initial acceleration.

Under good rail conditions this control can be left in the 'Full' (normal) position. The driver should:

■ Adjust the current limit setting to the maximum value that the locomotive is likely to develop without wheelslip, giving due consideration to the state of the rail at the time.

■ Move the power control handle at a rate depending on the type of train. The rate of moving the control handle controls the rate at which tractive effort is applied, up to the max set by the current limit setting.

Wheelslip

If wheelslip occurs the 'Wheelslip' light will be brightly lit and the output of the power unit will be reduced automatically as indicated by a

BELOW The driver of No. 50003 *Temeraire* shields his eyes from the bright sunlight during a shunting manoeuvre between trains.

BOTTOM The driver of No. 50033 *Glorious* climbs aboard his loco at Salisbury in January 1992.

reduction in current on the ammeter. If wheelslip ceases after the automatic power reduction, the light dims, and power is automatically and gradually restored.

No action is necessary unless wheelslip occurs persistently, in which case, move the current limit setting slowly in the decrease direction until wheelslip stops, apply the anti-slip brake, then advance the current limit setting again slowly, when track conditions improve.

While running

THE MAXIMUM SPEED OF 100MPH MUST NOT BE EXCEEDED.

Rheostatic brake

These locomotives were originally fitted with a rheostatic brake, in which the traction motors are automatically switched to function as generators, driven by the road wheels, and is intended to serve as a checking rather than a stopping brake.

The amount of rheostatic braking will depend on the speed of the locomotive and the position of the automatic air brake valve.

The current or power generated by the traction motor armatures when braking is dissipated across two banks of resistances and also supplies power to the motors of two fans for cooling these resistances.

It should be emphasised that this brake is an extra to the normal brake and, in the event of failure of the rheostatic brake, the locomotive is still classified as 'normal'. However, the failure should be reported as soon as possible, but it need not fail the locomotive.

Rheostatic braking operates automatically when a brake application is made through the automatic air-brake valve and the air supply to the brake cylinders exceeds 10lb/in^2. Under these conditions the rheostatic brake takes precedence over the locomotive air brake.

The rheostatic brake current is registered on the main ammeter and reaches a maximum of approximately 1,650 amps at 28mph. Below this speed the rheostatic brake current begins to fall away and is compensated by an increase in locomotive air-brake cylinder pressure. At approximately 10mph the rheostatic brake is automatically cancelled by the control equipment.

Train working

These locomotives are fitted with automatic air brake and vacuum train control and may be worked with vacuum-braked, unbraked or air-braked trains. THEY MUST NOT be coupled in tandem to locomotives fitted with vacuum-controlled air brake systems when working air-braked trains.

Brake indicator lights

Indicator lights are fitted in each cab and these indicate the position of the 'Air/Vacuum' switch, i.e. vacuum, air/passenger, etc., immediately after the battery isolating switch is placed to the 'On' position.

NOTE: Before coupling to an air-braked train the 'Air/Vacuum' switch should be moved to

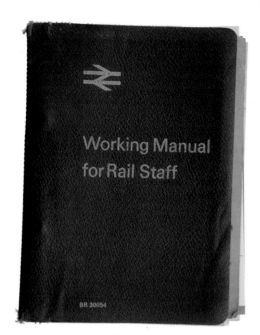

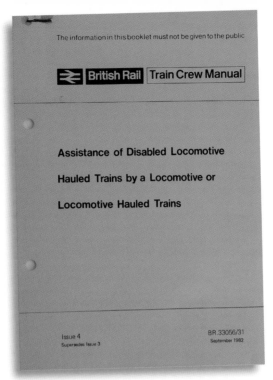

The information in this booklet must not be given to the public

≥ British Rail | Train Crew Manual

Assistance of Disabled Locomotive Hauled Trains by a Locomotive or Locomotive Hauled Trains

Issue 4
Supersedes Issue 3

BR.33056/31
September 1982

FAR LEFT BR 30054, the *Working Manual for Rail Staff*.

LEFT BR 33056/31, the *Train Crew Manual for the Assistance of Disabled Locomotive Hauled Trains by a Locomotive*.

the appropriate position, i.e. 'Air passenger' or 'Air goods', and before any attempt is made to move the locomotive again, all vacuum must be released from the chamber side of the locomotive by operating the vacuum-release valve. (One is fitted in each cab.)

Attaching the locomotive to an air-braked train

The sequence of operations when attaching a locomotive is:

- Ensure the 'Air/Vacuum' switch is in the correct position, then operate the 'Vacuum' release valve.
- Place driver's brake valve in 'Emergency' position.
- Connect the screw coupling.
- Ensure the auto air-brake pipe and main reservoir pipe isolating cocks are closed, i.e. in upright position on both locomotive and train.
- Couple the brake pipe and main reservoir (distinguished by 'Star' valve) pipe hose couplings. To couple the hose pipes, lift opposite couplings of the same type, placing the heads face to face at right angles and then, turning the heads downwards as far as possible, to fully engage the projecting edge of each head into the groove of the other head. Check that the heads are tightly engaged.
- Open the brake pipe and the main reservoir hose pipe isolating cocks (i.e. horizontal) on the locomotive and train.

- When the main reservoir gauge on the locomotive indicates the main reservoir has recharged to at least 118psi, place the driver's brake valve in the 'Release' position and note the brake pipe pressure builds up to 76psi. Place the driver's brake valve in the 'Running' position and note the brake pipe pressure leaks off to not less than 60psi (70psi nominal). This should take at least two minutes.

Testing train brakes

In all cases, as shown below and before the train is moved, it is important the auto brake valve MUST be placed in the 'Release' position

BELOW The driver of No. 50038 *Formidable* watches for the Right Away with a Penzance-bound service.

RIGHT No. 50041
Bulwark passes
Acton with a service
to Plymouth on 31
October 1988.

to charge the brake pipe to approximately
72.5psi, and so ensure the distributors assume
the correct position of the 'full release' of the
brake on the train. Then place in the 'Running'
position to allow the brake pipe pressure to leak
off to not less than 68psi (70psi nominal).

BELOW A
diagrammatic guide to
the driver's preparation
instructions for a
Class 50. *(British Rail)*

■ Attaching to train
  ♦ (1) Locomotive running round train.
  ♦ (2) Locomotive is changed.
  ♦ (3) Additional locomotive is attached.

■ Train formation is altered.
■ C&W depot test of train.
■ Guards continuity test.

Brake application

The auto brake valve handle must be moved
from the 'Running' to the 'First application'
position or beyond. Do NOT leave the handle
between these points.

It should be clearly understood, that in
addition to the conditions shown under 'Testing

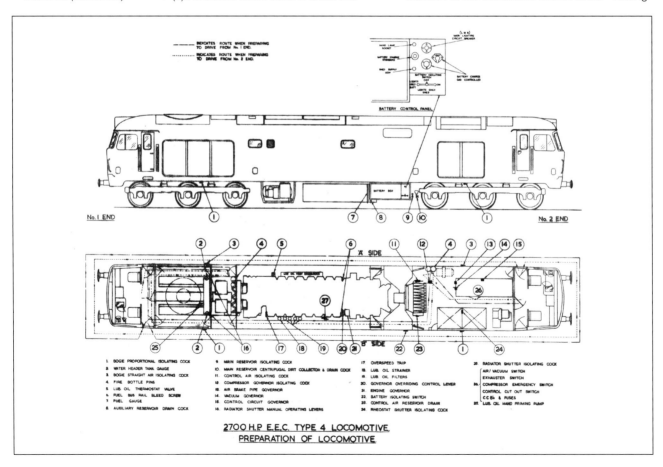

2700 H.P E.E.C. TYPE 4 LOCOMOTIVE.
PREPARATION OF LOCOMOTIVE.

Train Brakes' above, that when working a train and after any brake application or series of brake applications, the driver's brake valve must be placed in the 'Release' position for 15 to 30 seconds (dependent on the length of the train). This allows the brake pipe to be recharged to 72.5psi to ensure the full release of the brake on the train.

If at any time it is thought the brakes may be dragging – even if no brake application has been made – then the brake valve should be moved into the 'Release' position for 15 seconds or so, as above.

It is permissible to go from the 'Release' position to any 'Application' position, so long as the brake valve is returned to the 'Release' position when it is judged that the brake application has been completed. Failure to do this, i.e. returning the brake valve to 'Running' position, may result in some or all of the distributors remaining in the partially applied position, thus causing dragging brakes.

Detaching the locomotive

To detach the locomotive from the train, the following sequence of operations must be carried out:

- Ensure the brakes are applied on the train by the driver placing the brake valve in the 'Emergency' position.
- Close the coupling cocks of both ends of the two hose couplings between the locomotive and first vehicle.
- Uncouple the hose couplings by lifting and turning the heads to disengage them.
- Place the hose coupling heads in the retaining hoses (or dummy couplings if fitted).

- Disconnect the screw coupling.
- Move the 'Air/Vacuum' switch into the position required.

Locomotive lights

Switches are provided for the cab, engine room, train indicator panels, and tail lights etc. in each cab. In the event of an engine shutdown, whether driver-initiated or because of engine failure, all the lights will automatically go out after a period of 15 minutes. However, a supply will be maintained to the tail light circuit.

In order to restore the lights, the main lighting switch on the 'Battery isolating' switch should be turned off and then on again. This will ensure full lighting for a further 15 minutes.

Train heating

Provision is made for electric train heating by means of an 800 volt DC generator shaft driven from the main generator. This generator also supplies power for the radiator fan and pressurising fan motors.

If the locomotive is required to heat a train, the following procedure should be adopted:

- Check the train-heat light is 'Out'.
- Connect the screw coupling.
- Connect the necessary hose couplings, depending on the type of train to be worked.
- Remove locomotive and leading coach jumpers from their respective dummy sockets.
- Connect locomotive jumper into socket on leading coach and the coach jumper into the locomotive socket. Ensure both jumpers are secure and 'locked' in position. It is necessary to connect both jumpers and

ABOVE No. 50036 *Victorious* storms past the camera with a rake of NSE-liveried Mk1 coaches on the down main (westbound) through Hayes and Harlington..

insert the plug on the last coach into the dummy socket to complete the electrical circuit.
- Press the train-heat 'On' button and note the train-heat light is illuminated.

NOTE: The reversing handle must be in the 'EO' position and the engine running, if the locomotive is required to pre-heat the train. Approximately ⅔ full train heat will be available from the heating generator at idling speed.

During train working, should additional power be required for traction purposes, train heating may be switched off temporarily (i.e. climbing a steep incline). THE DRIVER MUST REMEMBER TO RESTORE THE HEATING AS SOON AS POSSIBLE.

To disconnect the locomotive after electric train heating, proceed as follows:

- Place the auto air-brake valve in the 'Emergency' position.
- Place the reversing handle in the 'EO' position.
- Press the train-heat 'Off' button and note the train-heat light is extinguished.
- Disconnect both heating jumpers and place them in their respective dummy sockets, making sure they are secure.
- Disconnect the necessary hose connections.
- Disconnect the screw coupling.

BELOW No. 50047 *Swiftsure* decelerates for a station stop on 24 July 1978.

Standard disposal duties

- Stop the locomotive by applying the auto air brake, and when the locomotive has been brought to a stand, place the auto air brake valve handle in the 'Emergency' position and wait until the brake pipe pressure drops to zero. Move the reversing handle to 'Off', then immediately stop the engine and remove the master key, then apply the handbrake.
- Check the straight air-brake handle is in 'Release' position, then place the auto air-brake handle in 'Running' position. Close cab windows and collect personal gear and place near the cab door.
- In non-driving cab:
- Apply the handbrake.
- Check windows and doors are closed.
- Return through engine compartment to driving cab. On returning to the driving cab, place the auto air-brake valve in the 'Shutdown' position, then release vacuum by operating the release valve in the cab.
- Report all known defects in the Repair Book.
- Switch off all lights, collect personal gear and close the cab door.
- Turn the battery isolating switch to 'Off'.
- Hand the control and door keys to the responsible person at the depot.

NOTE: All pipes are coloured for identification to assist when reporting defects, etc.
Colour identification of pipe lines:

Line	Colour	Symbol
Air, Compressor	White	A.C.
Vacuum	White	A.V.
Drainage	Black	
Electrical	Light orange	
Fire installations	Signal red	
Oil, diesel fuel	Light brown	
Oil, lubricating	Salmon pink	
Water, engine cooling	French blue	

Notes for the guidance of drivers when a fault occurs

If a locomotive shows only a slight reduction of power, no immediate action is necessary. A check on the equipment should be made at the next stopping point. If no obvious defects can be seen the journey may be completed.

If severe reduction of power occurs an

investigation should be made within five minutes at the most convenient stopping place. An immediate stop may be necessary if the shortage of power is accompanied by excessive vibration, noise or smoke from any part of the locomotive. If a period of coasting will allow the train to proceed to a booked stopping point, there is no need to bring it to a stand within five minutes, provided no serious defects are evident.

A shortage of power will probably be accompanied by a warning light becoming bright or an abnormal instrument reading. All indications should be noted before the train is brought to a stand. GREAT CARE MUST BE TAKEN TO ENSURE THAT NO SIGNAL ASPECTS OR LINESIDE WARNING BOARDS ETC. ARE MISSED WHENEVER INDICATIONS OR INSTRUMENTS ARE BEING CHECKED.

If a complete loss of power occurs, but the exhausters are still running, an attempt should be made to coast and bring the train to a stand under the protection of the next fixed signal.

In the event of a diesel engine shutting down in service, an application of the brakes will occur and the train should be stopped, if possible, at the next fixed signal.

When a train has been brought to a stand as a result of locomotive failure, and the necessary rules have been carried out, refer to the appropriate fault chart. This will show possible causes of trouble and indicate the action to be taken.

ABOVE The driver's view ahead from the cab of No. 50035 *Ark Royal*.

In some cases the possibilities may be numerous and the simpler defects should be checked before the more difficult ones.

When a cause for a defect can be definitely established and it is known that it can be corrected, inform the nearest signalman, station official or the traffic control, stating how long it will take to rectify the defect. Return to the locomotive and take the necessary action. When the defect has had attention, start the engine and make a test to ensure that traction power can be obtained and that auxiliaries function normally. The train may then be worked forward.

If any doubt exists as to the possibility of overcoming the fault, a fresh locomotive must be requested immediately. If the defective locomotive can only work forward on reduced power, arrangements must be made for a fresh

LEFT A heavily work-stained No. 50015 *Valiant* is seen at Exeter St David's with a Waterloo–Exeter service.

LEFT Original Network SouthEast-liveried No. 50025 *Invincible* rolls into Reading with a matching rake of stock.

locomotive to be provided at some point on the journey.

At the end of the journey the defect must be reported, and the full facts must be entered in the Repair Book. This will greatly assist the maintenance staff at the depot to where the locomotive is taken in identifying the cause of the defect.

To test fuses

Place the battery switch to 'Lights only' position. Remove fuse to be tested. Test fuse on fuse tester, which will be alive with the switch in this position.

NOTE: The fuse tester is not in circuit when the battery switch is in the 'Off' position.

With the battery switch in 'On' or 'Lights only' position, all lights except the tail lights will go out after approximately 15 minutes if the engine is stopped.

LEFT No. 50009 *Conqueror* was the 27th Class 50 to be refurbished and the 27th to be withdrawn.

BELOW No. 50022 *Anson* assists a failed InterCity 125 High Speed Train.

Fault lights

Fault	Desk fault light	Specific fault light
Low water	Red and blue until rectified	Blue until rectified (i.e. system topped up)
Water temperature	Blue until rectified or engine stopped	Blue until rectified or engine stopped (Note: Engine should be kept running as train heating generator supplies the radiator fan.)
Oil pressure	Red and blue until governor button is reset	Blue until governor button is reset
Low fuel	Blue until rectified	Blue until rectified (float switch operates at 200gal)
Blowers and pressurising fan	Blue until rectified or engine stopped	Blue until rectified or engine stopped
Overload	Remains blue until tripped by reset button	Remains blue until tripped by reset button
Earth fault	Blue while under power or rheostatic brake. Does not re-brighten once controller has been closed and re-opened	Remains blue until relay in the cubicle has been relatched by maintenance staff

Braking systems

Straight air and anti-slip brakes

The driver's straight air-brake valve in each cab is supplied from the locomotive main reservoirs and passes air at a pressure proportional to the movement of the brake valve handle through double check valves to a relay valve over each locomotive bogie. These valves draw air from the main reservoir supply and deliver it to the brake (locomotive) cylinders at a pressure proportional to that relayed to them from the straight air-brake valve.

If the driver wishes to make a partial locomotive brake application to check wheelslip, an anti-slip control on either driver's desk feeds an EP valve electrically, which then opens and passes air at $140lb/in^2$ (from the locomotive main reservoirs) via a $15lb/in^2$ limiting valve, into the straight air-brake system.

Automatic brake

The driver's automatic air-brake valves (one in each cab) control the normal braking of the locomotive and train.

When hauling a vacuum-fitted (or partially or non-fitted) train, the brake selector on panel 'A' of the control cubicle will be in a 'Vacuum' position. In this case, the exhausters will be running. Variations in pressure in the air-brake

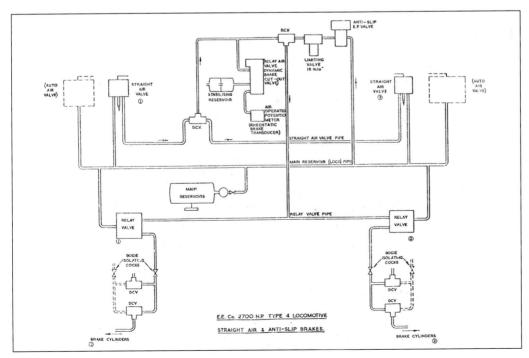

LEFT A diagram of the straight air and anti-slip brake system. *(British Rail)*

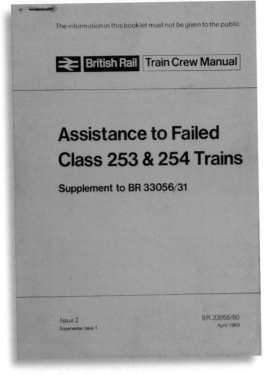

RIGHT BR 33056/80, the *Train Crew Manual for Assistance to Failed Class 253 and 254 Trains* (HSTs).

The information in this booklet must not be given to the public

British Rail | Train Crew Manual

Assistance to Failed Class 253 & 254 Trains

Supplement to BR 33056/31

Issue 2
Supersedes Issue 1

BR.33056/80
April 1983

pipe, initiated by the driver's auto-air-valve, are relayed to the VA1 control valve, which proportionately varies the vacuum in the vacuum brake pipe. This controls the train brakes directly and, through the distributor, the air brakes on the locomotive.

When hauling an air-brake-fitted train, the brake selector will be in an 'Air' position. The exhausters will not be working and the air-brake pipe pressure, controlled by the driver's auto-air-valve, will control all the brakes through the distributors on the locomotive, and on each hauled vehicle. The air-brake pipe is connected to the train through a 1in flexible connection towards the centre of each buffer beam. Unlike the main reservoir equalising pipe, there is no 'star' check valve in the air-brake pipe connection.

BELOW No. 50048 *Dauntless* departs from Bristol Temple Meads.

Vacuum passenger operation

The brake selector switch on panel 'A' of the control cubicle is set to 'Vacuum passenger'. Both exhausters will then run, providing the engine (and therefore the auxiliary generator) is running. In the event of one exhauster being defective, it can be cut out using the exhauster cut-out switch on the same panel. Only one compressor will run, No. 1 operating when the reverser is set for the locomotive to travel No. 1 end leading, and No. 2 operating, when set for No. 2 end leading.

In the event of the compressor in use becoming a failure, the other compressor can be brought into action by moving the compressor emergency switch on the same panel to an emergency position (No. 1 or 2 as the case may be).

The exhausters draw air through a vacuum restrictor valve in which the choke is operative in all positions of the driver's auto-air-valve except 'Release'. This restricts the suction on the vacuum brake pipe to ensure that a guard or passenger emergency brake application cannot be over-ridden.

The driver's auto-air-valve (port 4) is supplied with air at main reservoir pressure, and movement of the brake handle varies the pressure in the air-brake pipe (via port 5) from $70lb/in^2$ in the 'Running' position, to $72.5lb/in^2$ in the 'Release' position down to $46lb/in^2$ in the 'Full service' position. The air-brake pipe pressure acts, through a double check valve, on port 4 of the AV2 control valve (on the right-hand side of the Westinghouse frame).

Note:

■ The brake relay governor requires a pressure of at least $10lb/in^2$ from the distributor before it initiates rheostatic braking.

■ If the locomotive is braked using the driver's straight air valve, the rheostatic brake cut-out valve senses this (at port 10) and blocks the feed to the potentiometer, thus rheostatic braking is not available if the straight air brake valve is in use.

■ Rheostatic braking is cut out (electrically) at speeds of less than 10mph.

If the driver's auto-air valve is placed in the 'Emergency' position, the vacuum brake pipe (and air brake pipe) is directly vented to atmosphere providing an immediate full application of the brakes on the train, and through the distributor, on the locomotive.

If the driver's auto-air-valve is placed in the 'Release' position, the overcharge reservoir is filled with air at normal brake-pipe pressure. This operates the exhauster speed control governor, which operates contactors to speed up the exhausters and cuts out the choke on the vacuum restrictor valve. The full effect of both exhausters is then available to recreate brake pipe vacuum.

With both driver's auto-air-valves in the 'Shutdown' position, air at main reservoir pressure is supplied to the AV2 control valve (port 4). This renders the AV2 valve inoperative when the locomotive is being hauled or controlled by another.

An isolating cock is provided (just below and to the left of the AV2 valve) which, when closed, allows the locomotive to be worked as part of a vacuum-fitted train when no air pressure is available.

Vacuum goods operation

The brake-selector switch on panel 'A' of the control cubicle is set to 'Vacuum goods'. The same conditions will apply as described above for 'Vacuum passenger' operation, except in the supply of air to the distributor.

In both cases, the air brake timings EP valve (middle valve at the top of the Westinghouse frame) is 'de-energised-closed', but the restricted application EP valve (to left of air brake timings valve) is 'energised-open' for passenger operation only. Therefore, in passenger operation the air supply to the distributor (port 1) is via both chokes, but in goods operation it is via one choke only. The rate of application for the brake on an unbraked, partially or fitted train (when the selector should be in the 'Vacuum goods' position) is thereby restricted to reduce shocks in the train.

Air passenger operation

The brake selector switch on panel 'A' of the control cubicle is set to 'Air passenger'. The exhausters will not run but both compressors will run. The driver's auto air-valve varies the air brake pipe pressure as before, but in the absence of vacuum, the AV2 control valve is inoperative and the vacuum-operated isolating valve is closed.

This renders the air-controlled portion of the distributor (ports 2 and 3) operative.

With the brakes released, the distribution control reservoir (mounted with the release valve under the roof over the Westinghouse frame) is filled with air at $70lb/in^2$ via a charging choke in the distributor. On reduction of brake pipe pressure, the pressures at ports 2 and 3 of the distributor will be unequal. Air will then pass (from port 4), at a pressure proportional to the reduction in brake pipe pressure, to work the brakes (including the rheostatic brake) in the same way as when vacuum initiated.

Reduction in air-brake pipe pressure will be sensed by the distributors on the other vehicles of the train, and similar brake applications will be made.

Air goods operation

The brake selector switch on panel 'A' of the control cubicle is set to 'Air goods'. The same conditions will apply as described above for

ABOVE No. 50032 *Courageous* stands at Paddington in an atmospheric night-time study, on 13 January 1990. (*John Chalcraft*)

ABOVE No. 50032 *Courageous* stands at Paddington in an atmospheric night-time study, on 13 January 1990. (*John Chalcraft*)

BELOW In their latter days when Class 50s were operated double-headed, the preference was to attach the No. 1 ends together so that drivers could operate from the No. 2 ends, which were a less noisy environment to work in. Nos D400 and 50007 are seen so coupled here.

ABOVE **Double-headed Nos 50046 *Ajax* and 50011 *Centurion* cross Penadlake Viaduct near Bodmin with the 09.33 Penzance–Newcastle service on 28 August 1986. In this view, the locos are attached at their No. 2 ends.**

the 'Air passenger' position except that the passenger/goods changeover valve (top right-hand of the Westinghouse frame) is 'energised-open' when working goods trains.

Port 7 of the distributor is then fed with air pressure. This alters the brake application rate and the release timings (controlled by chokes within the distributor) to values compatible with those obtained on air-braked freight trains.

NOTE: The restricted application and air brake timings EP valves are both 'energised-open' when working air-braked trains (goods or passenger). A supply of air, unrestricted by chokes, is therefore available at port 1 of the distributor).

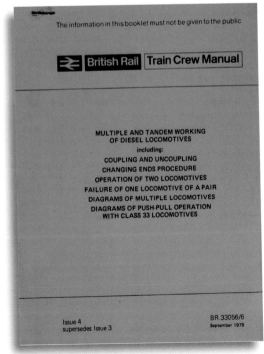

RIGHT **BR 33056/6, the *Train Crew Manual* for the Multiple and Tandem Working of Diesel Locomotives.**

Automatic air-brake release

The driver's auto air valve is connected by separate pipes to a reservoir divided into three compartments – 'equalising', 'overcharge' and 'rapid release'.

The equalising reservoir pressure responds proportionately to movement of the brake valve handle and then the pressure in the brake pipe follows suit until it has equalised. This arrangement eliminates unwanted pressure surges in the brake pipe.

When the driver's valve is moved to 'Release', the overcharge reservoir is charged with air at normal brake pipe pressure. This biases a diaphragm in the brake valve to raise the brake pipe pressure from 72.5 to 78lb/in^2. This assists in moving the distributors down the train to release the brakes. (The 70lb/in^2 limiting valve protects the locomotive distributor from this overcharge.) When the brake valve is returned to 'Running', the overcharge reservoir vents to atmosphere through a choke in the brake valve. This takes approximately five minutes, in which time the brake pipe pressure drops from 78 to 72.50lb/in^2. This is sufficiently slow to prevent unwanted brake applications on the train vehicle.

The rapid release reservoir is normally charged with air at brake pipe pressure. The connection between the two during release (and in brake application positions) is via a choke in the brake valve. Thus the pressure in the rapid release reservoir lags behind that in the brake pipe during release. This unbalance is sensed by another diaphragm in the brake valve and results in the inlet valve between the main reservoir and brake pipe being opened wider than would otherwise be the case. This assists the rapid release of the brakes with the auto-air-valve at 'Release' and in an application position, when partial release is required.

Experience on No. 50042 *Triumph*

To the author, Class 50s in Cornwall were the ideal motive power, when I was living in the county and travelling on the Plymouth–Penzance locals. Therefore, in later years, whenever we visited my wife's family in Cornwall I always visited the Bodmin & Wenford Railway to see the preserved No. 50042 *Triumph*. When I saw an advertisement for driver experience courses on 50042 it was therefore an ideal opportunity for me to try my hand at driving a 50 on the steep inclines of a Cornish branch line.

On the morning of the course I arrived bright and breezy at Bodmin General station and introduced myself. The first part of the day involved a briefing on the history of 50042 and the story of how it ended up on the Bodmin & Wenford. It was a small group of members of the railway who bought the loco, and while some of the larger preservation groups were awaiting the likes of celebrities Nos 50008 *Thunderer* or 50015 *Valiant* to come up for sale, this group had only limited funds so would have to bid for one of the already withdrawn 50s laid up in Ocean Sidings. Knowing that 50042 had a recently reconditioned engine, the group put in a bid and were successful in securing it.

The brief then turned to Class 50 technical information, the controls that I would need to know about as I would be operating them, and safety concerns. Once all that was over it was time to go out to the locomotive and get to grips with the controls. The engine was hand-cranked over 30 times by my instructor and then started up amid a spectacular cloud of clag! With the parking brake off, it was time to go.

Pulling out of Bodmin General light engine was relatively easy, even to a novice as it is level, so notch 1 was ample. After crossing a set of points more power could be applied and speed increased rapidly. I therefore eased off the power but the momentum was still sufficient to carry the loco up the 1-in-80 climb to Fitzgerald Sidings. There, I had to cut power and applied some straight engine brake to slow *Triumph* down to 5mph ready to cross a set of points. Once clear of the points, power could be applied again to reach the summit of the line where power was again cut ready for the descent to Bodmin Parkway.

The drop starts at 1 in 60, then levels for about half a mile. Then we began the descent proper at 1 in 40! In this direction the loco needed to be controlled by braking all the way down for about two miles. At the bottom is a 10mph speed restriction due to tight curves and points. Then, a little power was applied to roll into Bodmin Parkway station, where on the

other side of the platform is a main line station, so 50042's presence there makes it a rather special sight.

At Bodmin Parkway I did a bit of shunting in order to pick up a small rake of three Mk1 coaches which we would take up to General and bring back later in the day after lunch – a locally made Cornish pasty of course! The prospect of driving 50042 *up* the 1 in 40 with some weight behind it was going to be the highlight of the day!

Having eased over the points and around the tight curves, the line's maximum speed limit could be attained while going up the 1 in 40 with three on, so I gradually applied power and the loco unleashed a plethora of noise and acceleration. It was easy though, Class 50s used to take nine or more coaches heavily laden with holidaymakers and their luggage over the Luxulyan bank to and from Newquay. So, while this was impressive as a first driving experience for me, to *Triumph* it was child's play!

The iconic noise of a Class 50 under power kept on coming until I reached the line's speed limit and had to ease it back before we levelled out, but such an incline had given me a remarkable driver experience and a far greater understanding of the locomotive.

Since then I have also driven Nos 50007, 50015 and 50033, and while these were all fantastic experiences, the difference between them and taking 50042 up the 1-in-40 climbs of the Bodmin & Wenford have never been matched. And not only that, but it was also a 50 in Cornwall!

ABOVE No. 50042 *Triumph* fires up in dramatic style at Bodmin General on the Bodmin & Wenford Railway, ready for a day of driver experience training.

Tony Middleton's driving reminiscences

I started my railway career as a Traction Trainee/Secondman at Old Oak Common depot, London in October 1988. At that time, Class 50 withdrawals were slowly underway, with seven locos already having been taken out of traffic. I had only been at Old Oak for a few weeks when I found myself at the controls of a 50 for the first time. I was asked to move No. 50035 from the fuel point to the 'Factory' for a brake block change.

A week later, on 21 October, I coupled up and connected the multiple-working jumpers on Nos 50033 and 50034 in readiness for their use on the following day's 'Pennine Fifties' railtour. Despite these being the allocated locos for the train, I did try swapping NSE-liveried No. 50034 for large logo No. 50046. With No. 50033 also in large logo I figured it would have made a nice livery pairing, but unfortunately, Swindon Control was not playing ball. For a multiple working test I would get in the cab of one of the locos that was facing the cab of the other loco. With the 50s coupled together, I first applied the straight air brake followed by forward power. If the other loco started to pull away, you knew it was taking power. Likewise, with the controller in reverse, you knew the multiple working was operating correctly if the other 50 moved towards you.

From driving the locos on the depot, I

progressed to driving on the main line – providing the booked driver was amenable. Sometime during 1999 I recall driving No. 50031 and near Maidenhead the train reached a speed of 115mph. As we were approaching Burnham my regular driver said to me: 'Don't forget we have a booked stop at Slough.' I hadn't, and we stopped as booked.

Another memorable occasion that year was when I drove a Class 50 through my home town of Coventry. The service was the 1V41 Manchester to Paddington, which was booked a 50 forward from New Street. When the Old Oak driver offered me the driving seat on No. 50024 I didn't need a second invitation – and off we went. To this day, it is the only occasion when I have driven a 50 into and out of Coventry.

On 2 February 1989 I took No. 50003 light engine to Brentford to work the 6A54 refuse train to Appleford. This was in lieu of an unavailable Class 56. The 'Binliner' was loaded to 1,600 tonnes and although the driver insisted on performing his duties, I sat in the secondman's seat with my window wide open. No. 50003 put in a fine performance and managed to keep to time. After unloading at Appleford, *Temeraire* returned to Brentford with the 6A55 empties. Even that train weighed in at around 900 tonnes, but the 50 was more than up to the job.

Even as a secondman, I gradually got to know the characteristics of most of the locos. As with any locomotive, each one has its own character, whether this is its power application, responsiveness, braking – or merely an uncomfortable driving seat. Some were better than others. No. 50024 was a top machine to drive – as was No. 50025.

When Laira-based locos on the Waterloo–Exeter diagrams visited OOC for fuel and exams, I always enjoyed sampling them on the depot. Occasionally, they would find their way on to Paddington–Oxford services and my general recollection of them at the time was that most of them seemed to have a bit more power. No. 50018 was a particularly good Laira loco, having recently been fitted with a refurbished power unit.

In 1990, I passed out as a driver, but not on Class 50s. In October 1989, I was due to do the BR Class 50 driving course but a prior holiday commitment meant I was unable to

BELOW Tony Middleton is seen driving NSE-liveried No. 50024 *Vanguard* and large logo No. 50039 *Implacable* on to the Old Oak Common fuel point in March 1989. *(Darren Ward)*

attend. Unfortunately, due to the impending run-down of the class, this was one of the last driving courses for the type. However, all was not lost and I later passed as a Class 50 driver on the Severn Valley Railway – albeit only on heritage railways. It was to be another 12 years until I was passed for driving Class 50s on the main line!

One of the secondman duties involved working the 08.15 Paddington–Oxford and return, which was used to test locos off repair at OOC. Quite often this was a Class 50, and sometimes it was a Laira loco. On one occasion, Nos 50024 and 50039 were both on test on this train. I was driving the train on the return working from Oxford when the leading loco, No. 50024, failed with an engine fault. Fortunately, the battery voltage on 50024 was high enough to operate the locomotives' safety and electrical control systems. This meant that the locos could continue to work in multiple and I was able to use the controls of *Vanguard* to power trailing loco No. 50039.

I joined The Fifty Fund in 1993 and started working on No. 50044 at St Leonards depot in Hastings. More than two decades later, I am still involved with the group, which is now part of the Class 50 Alliance. The 50s had their flaws, as did most loco classes, although I had very few failures with them in BR service. I recall two flashover incidents: No. 50001 on a Paddington–Westbury, and No. 50024 on a Paddington–Plymouth. Fortunately, on both occasions the loco managed to soldier on without the train being terminated. Although flashovers were the Achilles heel of the class, there was a way of minimising them. When shutting off power, instead of simply winding the power handle back to the 'off' position, it was necessary to move it to 'notch one' for several seconds before moving it to 'off'.

During my BR career I managed to drive 43 of the class, the only ones that eluded me were early withdrawals Nos 50006, 50011, 50013, 50014, 50022, 50038, and 50047. The last Class 50s that I drove in BR service were Nos 50007 and 50033. The pair had arrived at Paddington on 19 February 1994 at the head of the 'Class 50 Memorial' railtour from Crewe. After fuelling at Old Oak Common, I took the two locos light engine from 'The Oak'

to Paddington station where a Plymouth driver was on hand to work the tour on to Exeter.

Although the class ended their main line operation under BR the following month, they returned to the main line in the post-privatised era three years later in November 1997. By then I was working with EWS, based at Acton and I was officially passed out for driving 50s on 10 August 2000. My first driving turns as a fully fledged Class 50 driver on the main line were various light engine and stock moves.

Having spent many years driving Class 50s in preservation it was a great feeling to be able to unleash the power on the main line without the restriction of a 25mph speed limit. On 21 December 2002, I had the pleasure of driving the 'Cornubian' railtour from Ealing Broadway to Bristol Temple Meads. Destined for Par, the tour featured Nos. 50031 and 50049 working in multiple.

One of the more quirky railtours I worked was the 'Silverlink Swansong Number 2' on 10 November 2007 which used No. 50049 and Class 37 No. 37410. I drove *Defiance* on the return from Bedford to Bletchley and then into Euston. Prior to that, I had taken No. 50031 into the same London terminus on the night of 28 August 2005 on an empty stock working off the 'Whistling Scotsman' railtour, which I worked forward from Rugby.

From a driver's point of view, the Class 50 cab is excellent and well soundproofed while the controls are well positioned – and they are free from draughts! Most importantly, the locos are responsive. Ultimately, however, the performance of a loco is dependent on how well it is maintained and Old Oak Common and Laira both seemed to do a pretty good job on them.

ABOVE Tony is pictured in the secondman's seat of No. 50023 *Howe* at Didcot East on a York–Paddington service in April 1990. The 50 had worked the train forward from Birmingham New Street. This locomotive carried the original NSE livery and received a repaint in the revised version at Old Oak Common in August 1989.
(Mark Brammer)

Chapter Four

The technician's view

With its complicated electronic equipment, the Class 50 must have caused considerable problems for the maintenance staff electricians that worked on them in the early years of operation.

OPPOSITE A fascinating scene from Old Oak Common as No. 50001 *Dreadnought* stands in the background with a partially dismantled engine. A lifting beam sits in the foreground.

ABOVE No. 50034 *Furious* has an engine lowered into place. *(British Rail)*

ABOVE Mechanics at Old Oak Common are seen at work while performing a piston change.

BELOW No. 50028 *Tiger* awaits a return to traffic following scheduled servicing at Old Oak Common in September 1987.

The Class 50 maintenance cycle is structured in defined classifications which are identified by the letters A to F. An 'A' Exam is the most minor while the 'F' Exam is a major overhaul. A description of the work required for each exam and the period between them is given here.

Maintenance classifications

'A' Exam	Carried out every 55 hours
'B' Exam	Carried out every 275 hours
'C' Exam	Carried out every 550 hours
'D' Exam	Carried out every 1,100 hours
'E' Exam	Carried out every 5,000 hours
'F' Exam	Carried out every 10,000 hours

'A' Exam

Fuel, water and coolant levels are checked and topped up as required. Any defects reported by the drivers are dealt with. Visual examination of the locomotive for obvious defects.

'B' Exam

Refuel, top up coolant, check toilet, fill screen washer bottle, clean marker lights and front yellow warning panel; clean internally.

With engine running

■ *Outside locomotive*

Check compressor oil level, buffer beam air connections, buffers, general examination of body and underframe including doors, roof hatches and battery boxes, overhead electric warning flashes in position, visual check of brake blocks and brake gear, visual check of bogie. AWS receiver, traction motor gearcase lubricating oil level, ETH jumpers and bogie split pins.

■ *Inside locomotive cab*

Carry out straight air brake test, automatic air and vacuum brake test, AWS test, check brake pipe pressure, driver's safety device, main reservoir pressure, windscreen wipers and washers, warning horns, blow-down brake equipment and operation of handbrake.

■ *Inside locomotive engine room*

Check engine governor oil level, engine

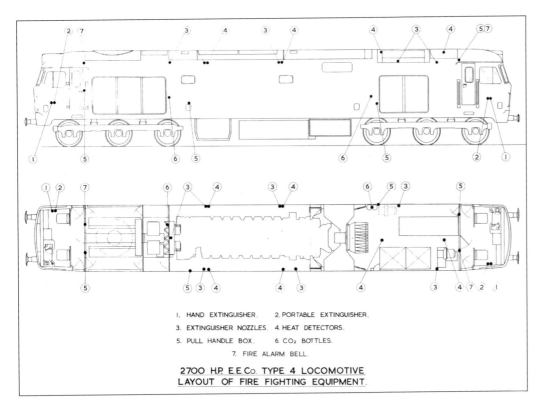

1. HAND EXTINGUISHER.   2. PORTABLE EXTINGUISHER.
3. EXTINGUISHER NOZZLES. 4. HEAT DETECTORS.
5. PULL HANDLE BOX.   6. CO₂ BOTTLES.
7. FIRE ALARM BELL.

**2700 H.P. E.E.Co. TYPE 4 LOCOMOTIVE
LAYOUT OF FIRE FIGHTING EQUIPMENT.**

coolant and lubricating oil sample, fire-fighting equipment, air filters, exhauster oil level, engine oil level and main fuel filter.

With engine stopped

Lubricate bogie moveable parts, handbrake mechanism and buffers.

Drain waste oil, check battery condition and fuses.

'C' Exam

Refuel, top up coolant, check toilet, fill screen washer bottle, clean marker lights and front yellow warning panel, clean cab front and side windows; clean internally.

With engine running

■ *Outside locomotive*

Check compressor oil level, buffer beam air connections, coupling, buffers, general examination of body and underframe including door and roof hatches, visual check of brake blocks and brake gear, bogies, lifeguards, hydraulic dampers, AWS receiver, wheels and tyres, traction motor gearcase seals, lubricating oil level, overhead electric warning flashes in position, ETS jumpers, traction motor electric connections and bogie split pins.

■ *Inside locomotive cab*

Test straight air brake, anti-slip brake, automatic air and vacuum brake, driver's safety device, AWS, warning horns, windscreen wiper and washer equipment. Check main reservoir feed pressure, air drain and blow-down systems, handbrake, fire extinguishers and lighting.

■ *Inside locomotive engine room*

Check turbocharger impeller blades, air filters, charge air coolers, engine coolant level, engine governor oil level, radiator unit for leaks and shutter operation. Take coolant and lubricating oil sample.

ABOVE Nos 50040 *Leviathan* and 50023 *Howe* bask in the sunshine at Old Oak Common.

fuel filters, engine fuel control linkage and engine exhaust manifolds.

'D' Exam

Refuel, top up coolant, check toilet, fill screen washer bottle, clean marker lights and yellow end; clean internally.

With engine running

■ *Outside locomotive*

Check compressor oil level, buffer beam air connections, coupling, buffers, general examination of body and underframe including doors and roof hatches, overhead electric warning flashes in position, AWS receiver, fuel strainer (filter), air reservoir automatic drain valves, clean outside of fuel tank and bogie split pins.

■ *Inside locomotive cab*

Test straight air brake, anti-slip brake, automatic air and vacuum brake, driver's safety device and hold-over button, AWS, warning horns, windscreen washers and wipers, air system blow-down equipment, main reservoir and brake pipe pressures. Check all desk indications and lighting.

■ *Inside locomotive engine room*

Check fuel pumps and injectors, air reservoirs and drain valves, low main reservoir

With engine stopped

■ *Outside locomotive*

Lubricate bogie moveable parts, handbrake mechanism, drawgear and buffers. Clean bogies and underframe, check condition of all six traction motors, both air compressors, drain waste oil, check battery condition and fuses.

■ Inside locomotive

Clean radiator elements and engine room floor. Check main generator, ETH generator, auxiliary generator, radiator motor, both traction motor blowers, both vacuum exhausters, exhauster oil level, vacuum limit valve, fuel supply equipment,

RIGHT A diagram showing the filling points on a Class 50. *(British Rail)*

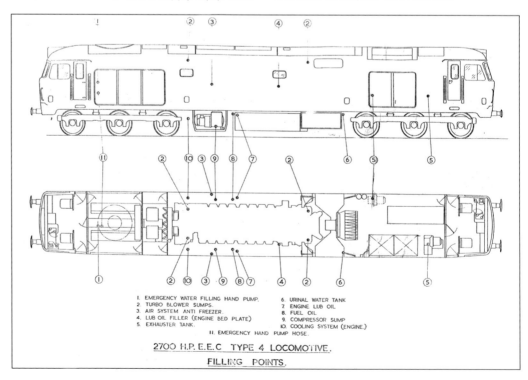

1. EMERGENCY WATER FILLING HAND PUMP.
2. TURBO BLOWER SUMPS.
3. AIR SYSTEM ANTI FREEZER.
4. LUB OIL FILLER (ENGINE BED PLATE)
5. EXHAUSTER TANK.
6. URINAL WATER TANK
7. ENGINE LUB OIL
8. FUEL OIL
9. COMPRESSOR SUMP
10. COOLING SYSTEM (ENGINE.)
11. EMERGENCY HAND PUMP HOSE.

2700 H.P. E.E.C TYPE 4 LOCOMOTIVE.

FILLING POINTS.

protection equipment, air vacuum brake valve, turbocharger, air filters, engine running speed, engine charge air, control air pressure, engine governor oil level, radiator unit for leaks and shutter operation, compressor governor, cooling water temperature unit, both vacuum exhausters and both traction motor blowers. Take coolant and lubricating oil samples.

With engine stopped
Lubricate bogie moveable parts, axleboxes, traction motor suspension bearings, handbrake mechanism, drawgear and buffers.

■ Outside locomotive
Check brake gear, traction motors and connections, traction motor gearcases, bogie equipment and connections, hydraulic dampers, wheel and tyre condition, battery condition, nose and jumper connections and both air compressors. Clean bogies, underframe and locomotive roof. Drain waste oil.

■ Inside locomotive cab
Check detonator and flag case, cab side window operation, cab door operation, fire extinguishers and handbrake operation.

■ Inside locomotive engine room
Check fuses, contactors, auxiliary switch equipment and relays, radiator group electrics, fuel supply motor, fuel injectors, engine valve gear and springs, camshaft, engine exhaust manifolds, main generator, auxiliary generator, train-heat generator, main ETH generator coupling, radiator fan motor, exhauster line filters, exhauster oil level, vacuum limit valve, air vacuum brake valve, compressor air supply, secondary air filters, fuel filters, lubricating oil level and fire-fighting equipment. Clean radiator elements.

'E' Exam
Refuel, top up coolant, check toilet, fill screen washer bottle. Clean marker lights and yellow warning end panel. Clean internally.

With engine running
■ Outside locomotive
General examination of body and underframe including doors, roof hatches and battery boxes, overhead electric warning flashes in

ABOVE A locomotive repair form for No. 50002 from October 1989, after it had been stopped at Laira for engine defects.

BELOW The scene inside the 'Factory' at Old Oak Common during 1987.

ABOVE No. 50021 *Rodney* at Old Oak Common with a 'not to be moved' flag in place during maintenance.

BELOW A Class 50 body on the jacks with bogies removed at Old Oak Common.

position, air reservoir automatic drain valves, visual check of brake blocks and brake gear. Check both air compressors, AWS, six traction motors and connections and bogie split pins.

■ *Inside locomotive cab*
Test straight air brake, anti-slip brake, automatic air and vacuum brake, driver's safety device and hold-over button, AWS warning horns, windscreen wipers and washers and air system blow-down equipment.

■ *Inside locomotive engine room*
Check fuel pumps and injectors, air reservoirs and drain valves, engine governor oil level, air system safety valve, air vacuum relay valve, exhauster efficiency, main reservoir pipe pressure, engine running speed, turbocharger and impeller, air filters, charge air coolers, control air pressure, radiator unit for leaks and shutter operation, water tank low-level switch, both vacuum exhausters, both traction motor blowers and fuel supply motor. Take coolant and lubricating oil samples.

With engine stopped
Lubricate all cab doors, windows and moveable parts, bogie moveable parts, axleboxes, traction motor suspension bearings, handbrake mechanism, drawgear and buffers.

■ *Outside locomotive*
Check compressors, buffer beam equipment, air connections, vacuum pipe, drawgear, buffers, brake gear, traction motor gearcase and bellows, wheels and tyres. AWS receiver, battery condition, nose-end jumpers. Clean outside of fuel tank, fuel strainer (filler), bogies and locomotive underframe. Drain waste oil.

■ *Inside locomotive cab*
Check power controller and master switch unit, detonator and flag case, track circuit operating clips, cab side window operation, cab door operation, fire extinguishers, handbrake operation and lighting.

■ *Inside locomotive engine room*
Check fuses, contacts, auxiliary switch equipment and relays, control cubicle, resistances, radiator group electrics, main generator, auxiliary generator, train-heat generator, exhauster filters,

exhauster oil level, vacuum limit valve, air/vacuum relay valve and isolating cock, compressor air intake, fire protection equipment, EP magnet valves, cooling water temperature control unit, compressor governor, turbocharger, fuel filter, engine oil strainer, fuel oil strainer, engine oil level, engine governor, engine governor oil strainer, engine camshaft chain, exhaust manifolds and internal coolant system pipes. Clean engine compartment, roof and radiator elements.

'F' Exam

As listed above, the 'F' exam is carried out every 10,000 hours and so is the most thorough of the examination categories. It consists of a virtual stripdown of the locomotive and includes major component changes such as the power unit and bogies, if required. The list of the work involved is too long to include here. The exam includes the complete testing of all equipment, and the locomotive could be out of traffic for up to three weeks. With the drawdown of the fleet, 'F' Exams on Class 50s ceased from April 1988.

Control system

Limitations of conventional locomotive control systems

On conventional diesel-electric locomotives, the master handle controls the power output using a 'closed-loop' control system consisting of the engine governor and load regulator. This system allows the driver to select the power output he requires, which is maintained to within close limits by the control system.

Starting a heavy train may require a current close to the operating value of the overload relays which, in turn, applies a tractive effort at the rails which may be close to the limit of adhesion. The master handle movement that the driver can use during starting and the initial acceleration period is limited because only a small amount of power is required to produce a high current when a train is stationary.

The Class 50 constant current system

The control system used on the Class 50 locomotives is designed to overcome the above limitations.

ABOVE No. 50039 *Implacable* on the jacks with bogies removed, at Old Oak Common.

BELOW A repair form for the power unit from No. 50007, receiving classified repairs in March 1987.

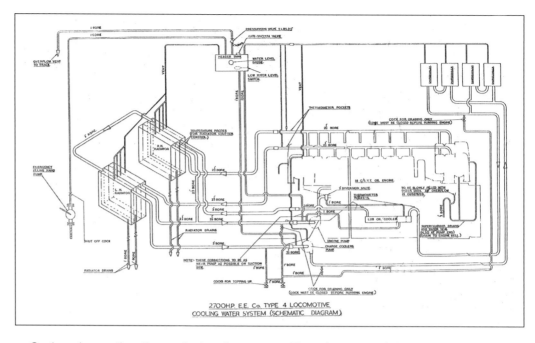

2700HP. E.E. Co. TYPE 4 LOCOMOTIVE
COOLING WATER SYSTEM (SCHEMATIC DIAGRAM)

On these locomotives the master handle controls both the power output and the traction motor current. The driver can, therefore, select the tractive effort he requires for starting and for the initial acceleration period. This setting is maintained by the control system until the power output corresponding to the master handle setting is reached, after which, acceleration continues at constant power until the balancing speed is reached. It must be noted that the selected current is not maintained to a constant value, but the value 'droops' as the speed increases, the reasons for which will be explained later.

The advantages of the above system can be summarised as follows:

- Under normal conditions the maximum generator current is limited to a value below the overload settings.
- It is no longer necessary to limit the power available at low master handle settings as this is automatically carried out by the current system. In notch 1 a maximum power of 640hp is available. This gives the driver a finer control of power output.
- The system is designed to allow full use of the master handle from standstill if required.

- The system readily lends itself to the addition of further controls and current limit, sensitive automatic wheelslip correction, and automatic slow speed control are incorporated.

Closed-loop control systems

All diesel-electric locomotives incorporate a closed-loop control system in the form of the engine governor and load regulator.

A control system requires a setting signal which is proportional to the required output, a reset signal which is proportional to the actual output, and an error or operate signal which is the difference between the required and actual signal, and is used to operate the control system. The 'required signal' must always be opposite in polarity to the 'actual signal'.

Operation of summing amplifier CA1

This unit consists of a multi-stage amplifier, with a voltage gain of approximately 100,000 times. The output voltage is limited internally to ±15V, which means that the input voltage required for maximum output voltage is ±0.00015V. The output voltage is always opposite in polarity to the input, therefore, an input voltage of -0.00015V will give an output voltage of +15V with respect to 22V.

Because of the extremely small input voltage required, the input terminals of the amplifier are sometimes called a 'virtual earth'.

When used as a summing amplifier, the input voltages to be 'summed' are applied to the amplifier via resistors RA and RB. The output of the amplifier is also connected to the input via R1.

Consider a positive voltage applied to terminal A and a negative voltage applied to terminal B, such that the resultant voltage applied to the amplifier input is negative. The output voltage will be positive and will be 'fed back' via resistor R1 to oppose the negative input voltage, and at some value of output voltage, the circuit balances. If the positive voltage on terminal A is increased, then the output voltage will reduce, to maintain balance.

The gain of the system depends on the values of the input and feedback resistors. A low value feedback resistor gives low gain, and low input resistors give high gain.

'Droop' feedback

When the output voltage of the CA1 amplifier is between 7V and 22V, additional feedback current can flow via R2 and D1, resulting in less gain. When the output voltage rises above 22V, D1 is reverse biased and the gain increases. This enables the amplifier output to more nearly match the generator characteristics.

Stabilising feedback

This network controls the rate of change of output voltage of the CA1 amplifier and consists of resistor R3 and capacitor C1. The resistance of R3 is fairly low and therefore, when the output

ABOVE A running repairs tool bag as carried on board The Fifty Fund's No. 50035 *Ark Royal*.

BELOW No. 50025 suffered a derailment on 14 August 1989 which caused such serious damage that it was not repaired. It was the 11th member of the class to be withdrawn.

voltage of the amplifier increases, additional feedback current flows until the capacitor is charged to the new value. Similarly, when the output voltage decreases, the capacitor discharges. In both cases the feedback current opposes the input voltage and controls the rate of change in output voltage to prevent hunting.

Control system components

The basic control system is comprised of the following components:

■ Driver's current setting potentiometer

This is operated by the master handle and gives a current setting signal to the control unit CU1. The setting is at maximum for master handle settings of 5 and above (60° movement).

■ Load limit potentiometer

This is operated by the vane motor connected to the engine governor and gives

a reset signal when the engine is fully loaded. The signal from this potentiometer is capable of opposing ALL setting signals.

■ Fixed reset signal

This signal is obtained from resistor R15 and is adjustable to limit the maximum current available from the system.

■ Regulating air valve

Operated by the master handle, this value gives an air signal to the governor to control the engine speed and therefore, also the power available.

■ DCCT reset signal

The voltage developed across resistor R4 is proportional to the highest traction current. One volt across R4 is proportional to 100A motor current.

■ Summing amplifier CA1

The amplifier sums the various input signals and gives an output voltage opposite in polarity to the resultant input. The output of the amplifier is between 7V and 37V with respect to battery negative, and is used to operate the generator load regulator.

■ Field supply unit KV10

This unit, together with its input unit NPE7-A9, varies the generator field current from 7A minimum to 140A maximum in response to signals from CA1. A 7V signal gives a minimum current and a 37V signal gives maximum current.

Basic current control system

When the driver opens the master handle, a current setting signal, corresponding to the handle position, is applied via resistor RA to the summing point. This signal opposes the fixed signal via RC, and the output voltage of CA1 begins to rise, with an appropriate increase in generator output. The traction motor current is measured by the DCCTs and a signal is fed back via RB to oppose the setting signal, until a balance point is reached at a particular current.

If this current is sufficient to start the train, the resulting traction motor back emf will cause a reduction in current (assuming the driver does not change the master handle position). To maintain the original current now requires an increase in generator excitation, but this can only occur due to a small reduction in current signal. The system, therefore, balances

---

BRITISH RAIL

MAIN LINE LOCOMOTIVE
CONTRACT REPAIR CONTROL FORM

To:Resident Engineer at: *CREWE*   for: *BREL*
Repairing Contractor: *BREL CREWE*

| | Home Depot *LA* | Region *WR* | Date *3/3/87* |

CLASS 50 POWER UNIT: IH 6968   *Ex Loco 50011*

Proposed Repair: Classified/UnClassified/Rectification/Special

Recieving Region (If transfer via works: | Shopping Authorised On: *4 3 87*
    by: *Jms Stephens.*

REPAIR SECTION

INPUT			DAY ONE DATE	CONTRACT DAYS			RELEASE DATES			Repair Output Days (+/−)
PLAN DATE	ACTUAL DATE	DELAY IN DAYS		Fixed for Repair Code	EXTRA AGREED	TOTAL	To Trial	Planned	Actual	
							To Traffic			

| Accepted for Contractor by: on: | Repairs Authorised by Resident Engr for BR by: on: |
| Certified Complete (Ready for trials) by: on: | Accepted by Resident Engr (Ready for trials) for BR by: on: |

TRIALS SECTION (When applicable)   note:-1st trial run day incl in contract days, as above

Date for Trial :		Post Trial Attention :								Correction
on	off	DAY ONE	Release date Planned	Actual	DAY ONE	Release date Planned	Actual	DAY ONE	Release date Planned	Actual	Days Debit
on	off									
on	off									

FINAL OUTPUT DAYS (Credit/Debit +/−)
Repair :−   TOTAL +/−
Trials & Attention :

| *REPAIRED LOCOMOTIVE* :− Certified complete, ready for traffic by Contractor:−   date:− | *REPAIRED LOCOMOTIVE* Final acceptance by Resident Engr for B.R. by:−   date:− |

| *COMPLETION OF DOCUMENT* Accepted by Resident Engr for B.R. by:−   date:- | Finalised copies to:- R.M&EE (Owning Region) − 2 Contractor/HQ (As Reqd) Resident Engr (As Reqd) |

FAR LEFT KV10 (CU3) and filter panel (CU3b).

LEFT A close-up of the KV10 equipment.

at a slightly lower current. This current 'droop' continues as the locomotive accelerates and this is a characteristic of the system.

Basic power control system

The above current control system operates during the initial acceleration period up to approximately 15mph. At this speed the engine becomes fully loaded and the load limiting potentiometer operated by the governor applies a voltage to the summing point, which, together with the signals from R15 and the DCCT signal, oppose the driver's setting signal to control the power.

Until this point is reached the LLP has been resting in the zero voltage position. As the acceleration continues, LLP applies an increasing 'reset' voltage to keep the power constant. Note there is no droop with the power control system and the engine governor controls the generator output in response to the regulating air pressure.

Power delay circuit

When the master handle is in the 'Off' position, a positive voltage is applied via MUR to the CA1 amplifier to ensure that the generator field is at minimum when power is taken.

The operation of the load regulator is delayed by about half a second when the master handle is moved from the 'Off' position. To avoid instability a slightly longer time delay is included in the control system. This is provided by capacitor C9 which discharges slowly when GFC1/1 interlock opens, to allow the control system to operate.

Also included in this part of the circuit is an FCR interlock which closes each time a field divert is taken to reduce the generator excitation, thus reducing the amount of engine overload. This relay is inoperative after the third field divert has operated, to prevent FCR from operating at the final high speed unloading point, which occurs between 80 and 100mph.

Current limit potentiometer

The driver can set the current he requires for starting and for the initial acceleration period by moving the power handle between positions 1 and 5. In certain circumstances it may be convenient to limit the maximum current available and this can be achieved by using the current limit potentiometer.

When the driver's setting is more positive than the current limit setting, the diode is reverse biased and the current limit has no effect. If the master handle is now moved to the maximum position and the current limit is in the half position, the diode is forward biased and current flows through resistance R. The difference in setting voltages appears across resistance R, and the actual setting voltage at point A equals the current limit setting plus the volt drop across the diode.

Field divert fixed setting signal

After the first field divert has operated, a fixed setting of 16.4V is applied to the CA1 amplifier. This signal over-rides the driver's setting and the current limit setting. This signal can only be opposed by the LLP (and FCR when the next field divert is taken). The driver can still control the locomotive and power with the master handle. If a lower power is required, the driver reduces the master handle setting with a corresponding reduction in regulating air pressure. The governor reduces the engine speed accordingly and LLP moves to give a more positive reset voltage and, therefore, lower power.

The fixed setting signal limits the maximum current in weak field to 2,400A but more importantly, by setting this signal it ensures that field reversion can take place, even if the driver's master handle setting corresponds to a current lower than the operating value of FDR.

BELOW No. 50033 receiving engine repairs on 10 February 1992. The A1 cylinder liner is nearest the camera. *(Paul Furtek)*

BOTTOM No. 50043 *Eagle* is seen outside Old Oak Common depot.

Automatic wheelslip correction

The wheelslip amplifier circuit is called an integrating amplifier. The diode connected between the input and output prevents the output voltage falling below 22V. The resistor and capacitor control the rate of rise in output voltage, in a similar way to the stability circuit on CA1. The important characteristic of this circuit is that the rate of rise in output voltage depends on the magnitude of the input voltage.

The input voltage depends on the amount of wheelslip and therefore, a large amount of wheelslip will cause a rapid rise in output voltage, to give a quick connection.

When wheelslip is arrested the input voltage disappears and the amplifier is reset slowly by a high value resistor connected to the 44V supply. This ensures that power is restored gradually and reduces the possibility of further wheelslip.

Engine loading control

This circuit has been included in the control circuit to prevent the slight hunting which occurred if the driver moved the master handle quickly from position 1 to position 7. Any sudden increase in master handle setting will cause a current to flow through the diode to charge a capacitor. A voltage will, therefore, be applied to the wheelslip amplifier until the capacitor is charged. This simulates wheelslip and the amplifier output voltage applies a reset signal to CA1 until the capacitor is charged to the new value.

Traction motor current measurement

The traction motor currents are measured by three DCCT's connected to the supply cable of each pair of motors. The supply for the DCCTs is taken from an alternator driven by the fuel pump motor.

The DCCTs perform the following functions on the Class 50 locomotives.

- Give an isolated reset voltage proportional to the highest traction motor current to the main control amplifier CA1.
- Give a voltage proportional to total generator current to the cab ammeters which are calibrated to read generator current.
- Derives a voltage proportional to the difference between the average motor

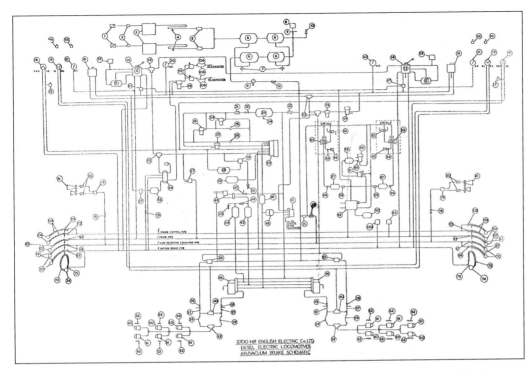

LEFT A schematic diagram of the Class 50's air/vacuum brake system. *(British Rail)*

current and the highest motor current. This voltage is fed to the wheelslip amplifier CA2.

Operation of DCCTs

To fully understand the operation of the DCCTs requires a sound knowledge of magnetic and alternating current theory. The following description is somewhat simplified and for those readers who may wish to obtain more details, the subject is well covered in the various text books available on 'Magnetic Amplifier'.

The following characteristics of the components of a DCCT must be understood:

■ Magnetic saturation

When current is passed through a coil wound on an iron core, a certain flux density will be produced in the core. If the current is increased, the flux density will increase at the same rate until a point is reached where further increase in current produces no further increase in flux density. At this point the core is saturated. The iron used in the DCCTs changes from the unsaturated to the saturated condition for a small increase in current when the saturation point is reached. Iron cores used in transformers saturate gradually.

■ AC current in an inductance

When an AC voltage is applied to a coil with an iron core, the current waveform lags the voltage waveform by a quarter of a cycle. This is due to the back emf in the coil which opposes the flow of current; therefore, the current is maximum when the back emf is minimum and zero when the back emf is maximum.

■ AC current in a resistive coil

If the iron core was removed from the above coil and the same voltage applied, the current would increase in value and also become almost in phase with the voltage.

■ Simple transductor

Consider the above AC coil with an additional DC coil wound on the same

BELOW No. 50046 *Ajax* awaits attention at Laira.

core with the same AC voltage applied. If a small DC current is flowing in the second coil, at some point near to the peak of the AC waveform, the combined effect of the AC and DC current will saturate the core, causing a sudden increase in AC current. When saturated, the core has no controlling effect on the AC coil current, until the total current falls below saturation point. If the current is increased, saturation occurs earlier in the AC waveform.

The AC current flowing is, therefore, proportional to the DC current over the working range of the transductor.

A limitation of the above simple circuit is that the two coils on the iron core also act as a transformer and therefore an AC current is induced into the DC winding.

BELOW A locomotive repair control form showing that No. 50012 *Benbow* needed its main generator changing in December 1988, but stating the subsequent withdrawal of the loco in January 1989.

Practical transductor

There are various methods of preventing AC current flowing in the DC winding, the most common method being to use two identical 'Transductors' connected so that the induced AC currents in the DC winding oppose each other. An added advantage of this system is that one core will saturate on positive half cycle and the other on negative half cycle, therefore producing a symmetrical current waveform.

DCCT circuit

In this case the DC windings consist of the single cable passing through the centre of the cores.

The transformation ratio of the DCCT is 2,000:1 and the outputs of the three DCCTs are connected three 5:1 ratio current transformers. The overall ratio is therefore 10,000:1.

Greatest and average current circuits

The three bridge rectifiers B1, B2 and B3 automatically select the greatest traction motor current. This greatest current flows through three 100 ohms resistors R3, R4 and R5. Therefore, IV drop across each resistance corresponds to 100A traction motor current. The voltage across R4 is used as a reset signal for the control system. Since this is proportional to the greatest current, the control system will automatically limit the current if a pair of motors are isolated. In other words, the control system does not operate on total generator current but on highest traction motor current.

The summation transformer provides a current proportional to the average traction motor currents and this operates the cab ammeters.

Wheelslip signal

The difference between the greatest and average signals is developed across resistors R5, R6 and R7 and is used as a wheelslip signal.

A fitter's recollections

Former Laira fitter Mike Woodhouse describes his time working on Class 50s in these extracts from his 1990 book of memoirs, *Blood, Sweat and Fifties*.

Hard day's night

"It is Friday, 31 August 1984; the time is 10.30pm. For most people it is the end of

RIGHT **The restoration of No. 50033 during March 1994 for presentation to the National Collection involved the replacement of corroded bodywork.**
(Paul Furtek)

the working week and the end of the day, but for those of us on the night shift at Laira the hard graft is just about to start. It is a clear but mild summer's night, still with a lingering remainder of the heat of the day. I book on for duty, and after changing into overalls I'm ready for work.

"The Servicing Shed Foreman informs me that tonight I will be working mainly on Class 50s: seven are awaiting attention, together with one Class 45 and one Class 47. It should be borne in mind that there are two departments concerned with keeping locos running at a depot such as Laira, namely Traffic and Movements, plus the CMEE (Chief Mechanical and Electrical Engineer – in other words, repair and maintenance). Both must work hand-in-hand to achieve optimum results.

"After collecting my tools and lamps I make my way to No. 4 road in the main shed. The work will be carried out by a gang of two fitters, one electrician and a mate. 47053 is on the fuelling point topping up with only 26 gallons of fuel; while this is in progress I make a quick detour to survey the scene in the rest of the shed. There are seven Fifties out of service, these being:

- No. 1 road: 50032 (OC), on jacks for a double bogie change
- No. 4 road: 50021 (OC), flashover repair to main generator
- No. 5 road: 50014 (LA), 'B' exam
- No. 6 road: 50012 (LA), 'B' exam;
- 50017 (LA), repair to ETH generator
- Outside: 50015 (LA), awaiting transfer to Doncaster Works
- Cleaning shed: 50044 (LA), 'B' exam

BELOW **Depot Engineer Malcolm Wishart supervising some of the apprentices as they put the finishing touches to No. 50033** *Glorious*, **ready for its handing over to the National Railway Museum, albeit a reluctant recipient!** *(Paul Furtek)*

RIGHT **On 17 March 1994, Laira fitter Chris Reece refits the** *Fearless* **nameplates as No. D400 is transformed into large logo No. 50050 for the final Class 50 railtours.** *(Paul Furtek)*

ABOVE No. 50007 on the jacks at Laira minus bogies, waiting to receive replacements from No. 50046, which can be seen raised on jacks in the background, on 10 February 1992.
(Paul Furtek)

"Now it's back to my night's work, which will consist mainly of footplate checks and the basic 'A' exam to seven Fifties, most of which are already allocated to work trains the next morning. These are:

50048 (LA)   'A' exam, booked on Turn 213b: 05.38 Plymouth to Penzance (23.57 ex-Paddington); 11.05 Penzance to Paddington, etc.

50046 (LA)   'A' exam, booked on Turn 211c: 07.07 Plymouth to Paignton empty stock; 09.45 Paignton to Paddington, etc.

50019 (LA)   FP exam, booked on Turn 220b: 04.05 Laira to Exeter empty stock; 05.48 Exeter to Waterloo, etc.

50016 (LA)   FP exam, booked on Turn 221b: 05.40 Laira to Newton Abbot staff train and local to Exeter; 08.13 Exeter to Waterloo, etc.

50025 (OC)   FP exam, booked on Turn 205d: 06.08 Laira to Paignton empty stock; 08.55 Paignton to Paddington, etc.

50045 (LA)   FP exam, spare, confined to local duties; awaiting transfer to Doncaster Works for classified repair.

50010 (LA)   Due to arrive with loss of coolant problems.

"These locos would clock-up over a thousand miles between them whilst hauling the Summer Saturday holiday traffic, and it is our responsibility to see that they perform it without any mishap. It will be a busy night.

"47053 has now come on to the pit for its inspection. 50048 draws up to take fuel, and as it has been out on the road for some time it takes on 745 gallons. The whole area is lit up by tower arc lamps making it just like daylight. 50046/016/010 have already arrived and, engines running, are waiting for their turn at the fuelling point. My mate and I start on 50048's 'A' exam, and though not long back in service it looks a little grubby. I do the bogie examination first and note that all the brakes need adjustment. I then join my mate in the cab for a full brake test and engine run-up.

"Meanwhile, 50046 has drawn up and proceeds to fill up with 270 gallons of diesel. I give the movements men the all-clear for 47053 and 50048, and as it is now midnight we have a drink of tea while the two locos are moved out and replaced by '46.

"On our return nothing has happened, the locos are in the same place as before. The reason is that the shunt crew on 08895 are busy drawing the chained-together old bogies out from under 50032 and depositing them in the next road, followed by collecting the replacements and reversing the procedure so that the loco can be reassembled. Outside 45012 is ready for the Plymouth to Penzance parcels, and a buffet car required at Penzance is being attached. By now *Ajax* is in place over the pit and we begin its 'A' exam. Again, the brakes need adjustment and the windscreen wiper on the secondman's side is found to be broken and in need of replacement.

"We are working against time, and to add to the difficulty there appears to be confusion concerning 50010, which has drawn up to take fuel: obviously the Movements side are not aware of its loss of coolant problem. In any event, 50021 is already berthed in No. 4 road, and has been there for a week with its flashover damage, meaning that space is at a premium. Therefore it is decided to concentrate on locos with booked workings later on in the day.

"50025 manoeuvres up to the fuelling point, and we examine the brakes while they are on: once more adjustment is needed. In the interim, *Invincible* has taken on 260 gallons of fuel. There is still no sign of 50019 arriving back at Laira after its day's labour, yet according to the plan, it should be the first to be booked off again in the morning. As we complete the checks on '25 I notice that '32 is being lowered on to its new bogies and across the other side of the shed the overhead crane is lifting the replacement ETH generator into '17.

"It is now 2.30am and we take our meal break. 50016/019/045 remain to be serviced, along with 50010 if we can find time. During our absence, '25 plus '46 are shunted out and '16 plus '45 shunted in.

"*Barham* takes 577 gallons of fuel and *Achilles* 299 gallons. Looking over the former it is found that very little attention is needed, whereas the latter needs its brakes adjusting. This done, I tell my mate that I will go and have a look at '10 whilst the next shunt is completed. It had arrived after piloting 50035 on the up sleeper (21.35 Penzance to Paddington). I check the coolant level first and find this to be satisfactory, and so check the radiator and engine for leaks; again nothing amiss. Next, I examine the radiator fan speed, as perhaps the coolant had boiled away. Once more this was

not the problem, and so I return to No. 4 road where 50019 is just arriving.

"As stated earlier, *Ramillies* is booked off at 04.05, but, surprise surprise, the brakes need adjusting. I decide I had better report to the foreman about both '10 and '19, as it might well prove preferable for the latter to swap duties with another 50 already available. Unfortunately, this will not be possible as Movements have

ABOVE No. 50007 undergoing a power unit swap with No. 50046 on 23 December 1991. *(Paul Furtek)*

LEFT Following the mechanical part of the overhaul of No. 50007, the loco was sent on a light-engine run in grey primer, from Laira to Newton Abbot and back, on 12 March 1992. This was the only main line outing of the loco prior to repainting and it is seen after its return to Laira. *(Paul Furtek)*

ABOVE A gathering of depot staff with Geoff Hudson at Laira with Nos 50007 and D400 providing the backdrop.

committed 50019 to train 5002, the ecs for the first up Waterloo service. Time is not on our side and the eyes are getting a little heavy. The engine needs 25 gallons of oil, and by now the Exeter crew are standing by and have to wait for us to finish the exam.

"Our foreman returns to tell us that 50010 will come in on No. 4 pit behind 50021; we will have a second look for coolant leaks. The final shunt is made and '19 leaves the shed trailing smoke, clouding the light of the shed lamps. *Monarch* arrives, and a glance at the bogies reveals the need for a complete reblock. Again, this is relayed to the foreman, who says that '10 will be stopped for further investigation.

"It is now the time to write up the logs and worksheets. The TOPS computer shows that Laira's 50027 is stopped at Tyseley for derailment damage, whilst 50029 – also one of ours – is on Old Oak Common for a main generator change. It is now 5am and time for

a wash before booking off and going home to bed. 'Good morning, Fifty followers, I hope you all enjoy your Summer Saturday travels.' Perhaps next time you will spare a thought for those nightshift men who prepared your locos for traffic."

Day return to Penzance

"It was a warm summer's afternoon, the date sometime in 1975 or 1976. After booking on at Laira at 14.30 I was told I was to take the stopper to Penzance, in order to monitor 50002 which was suffering from engine stopping faults. The loco had just been transferred from Old Oak Common, and typically for the machines not long off the LMR, it was in a rather grubby condition. Of course, at the time '02 was unnamed and unrefurbished. After obtaining tools and a tea can I made my way to No. 6 road where the loco stood outside the shed, ready for its booked turn, 2C74, the 16.45 off Plymouth.

"The cab interiors were in a poor state, dirty and showing some corrosion to the desk fittings, possibly indicating that the loco had lain out of use for a long time. The reason became obvious when I entered the engine room, as a new main generator had recently been fitted at Crewe Works. Before setting off I checked the levels of coolant, engine sump oil and engine governor oil. The four-character headcode was still operational, and when I confirmed the train reporting number with the crew this was rolled up to order. The engine was started and final checks made. There was time in hand, and so the driver suggested we move off shed early and make a cup of tea at North Road station.

"The 16.45 was usually made up of five coaches, and was primarily used by schoolchildren and shoppers from East Cornwall. It called at all stations, including the Halts at Dockyard, Devonport, Keyham and St Budeaux, and then all points west. The guard's whistle blows and we pull out on time. 50002 ambles along past the naval dockyard, where I notice a large collection of surface ships and submarines, all with names, but as yet, no association with the Fifties. On towards the Royal Albert Bridge spanning the River Tamar; a brake application is made to bring our speed down to the required 5mph. Halfway across and we are in Cornwall.

"There is no sign of any faults yet, but I don my earmuffs and disappear into the engine room to observe as power is applied after the Saltash stop. Oil pressure remains steady at 60psi. The heat thrown out from the engine is breath-taking, with the exhaust pipes glowing cherry red: one set of pipes is white hot, indicating the engine timing is out, a point to be booked. All the turbochargers are working together at 9psi. As yet there is nothing to indicate the cause of the shutdown problem, and so I go out past the dirty inertia air filters and take in the fresh, cool air.

"We continue our journey westwards, running into the setting sun, which suggests it will be a fine day tomorrow. Arrival at the Penzance terminus is scheduled for about 7pm, and we approach the station a few minutes down. I resolve to inform Laira of the position on arrival, as the next leg of 50002's diagram is 1A01, the 21.35 up sleeper throughout to Paddington.

We are greeted by the station supervisor who says we are to take 50035 back with us in multiple as far as Plymouth, as it is suffering a low power fault which will need to be rectified at Laira. It is agreed that we will run-round to the flower bay under the sea wall and collect '35 and then couple on to 1A01 before having our tea break. The Penzance Class 08 pilot shunts the train, and then the pair of Fifties (connected in multiple) back on and their engines are shut down. Now it's time for tea.

"I decide to go around both locos and check all oil and coolant levels prior to departure. By now the sun has sunk into the Atlantic, and the passengers are on board for their nocturnal journey to the Metropolis. We ease out of the station gently with theoretically 5,400bhp and a trailing load of 12 for 470 tons. 50002's engine shuts down; we restart and I go into the engine room. The engine stops again. A second restart is made and we struggle into St Erth. I inform the driver that it appears to be an electrical fault now that we are working in multiple. We therefore decide to uncouple the multiple jumper cables, using '35 to provide the ETH only and '02 for traction. 50002 picks up its train with a struggle, now pulling an extra 117 tons as well as the heavy train. Fortunately there is no more trouble from 50002, and so there must be a jumper fault on one of the locos.

"The problem now is that we are losing time. As our secondman is a passed Class 50 driver the decision is taken to use '35 for tractive power but driven from its own cab; in other words working the Fifties in tandem, not in multiple. Now it is right away to Plymouth with no further mishaps, '02 working well and '35 limping on its low power. At last Devon is reached, and as we pass Saltash we have a clear view of the Royal Albert Bridge all lit up. The night is clear and starlit, and this gives reflections in the water at the dockyard. On the final approach to Plymouth the signal is against us and we stop, before the yellow aspect shines and the route indicator displays Platform 7. We are 15 minutes down. Our duo are detached whilst 50004 waits patiently in Platform 8 to take 1A01 forward. We slip out of the lights of North Road station and I get ready to see our duty foreman and then sign off."

FLASHOVER!

By Joseph Burr, Chairman of The Fifty Fund

It has long been accepted that the Achilles heel of the Class 50 is its main traction generator (English Electric generator Type EE840/4B). Of the fleet of 50 locomotives, 13 were finally withdrawn due to generator failures and the costs associated with repairs.

There is something of a widely held misunderstanding that all (or most) Class 50 generator failures and subsequent locomotive withdrawals classified as a 'generator fault' were as the result of flashovers.

While Class 50s do suffer flashovers, they are by no means the only generator failure mode and although quite dramatic, they are only occasionally serious enough to require removal to effect a repair. Other issues such as earth faults (insulation failures) in the series fields are normally much more difficult and expensive to fix, and therefore were more frequently the reason for loco withdrawal.

But let's look into things more deeply by asking the question: what is a generator? Simply, it is a device for making direct current electricity. Think of it like a battery, but instead of using a chemical reaction to make the electricity, it uses mechanical rotation combined with magnetism. Like the battery, it has a positive and a negative terminal, but unlike a battery we can change the output voltage by changing the strength of the magnetic field. The strength of the magnetic field is controlled by varying the electrical current in the coil of wire mounted to the stationary frame of the generator called the field winding.

A flashover, as defined by Professor Malcolm Bradford of Sheffield University, is 'an unwanted or uncontrolled electrical discharge between electrical conductors or between a single conductor and earth'. Other notable worthies define it as 'an electrical discharge over or around the surface of an insulator'. It might help if we unpick some of the jargon in these sentences.

- ■ An electrical insulator is something that keeps electricity at different voltages (or potentials) apart. It does not have to be anything special and quite often air is used. Look at the 400,000 volt national grid cabling mounted on pylons; it's just air stopping the electricity from jumping between the cables.
- ■ A conductor is something that electricity will flow along. Most conductors in regular use are made of copper, as this metal efficiently passes the electricity and in doing so does not heat up as much as other materials.
- ■ Electrical discharge is when the electricity finds it easier to pass between conductors and jumps through the air, rather than going another way round through the conductors. This jumping stream of electricity heats up the particles it hits, creating a glowing arc.
- ■ Earth. Literally the voltage of the ground (planet Earth), but engineers do use the term to mean the prevailing voltage of the return half of a circuit.
- ■ One more term we need to understand is a circuit. In the Class 50 context, this is the route the electricity will move along from the source (the generator) through the control system, the traction motors and back to the other end of the generator.

The weak point of the Class 50's main generator, like most large DC motors and generators, is the area around the commutator – this is the part of the generator that passes the generated electricity from the rotating part, where it is made in the rotating windings, to the stationary frame so it can be used.

BELOW A simple DC generator.
(Joseph Burr)

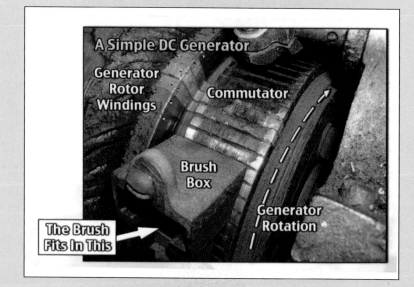

A Simple DC Generator

Generator Rotor Windings

Commutator

Brush Box

Generator Rotation

The Brush Fits In This

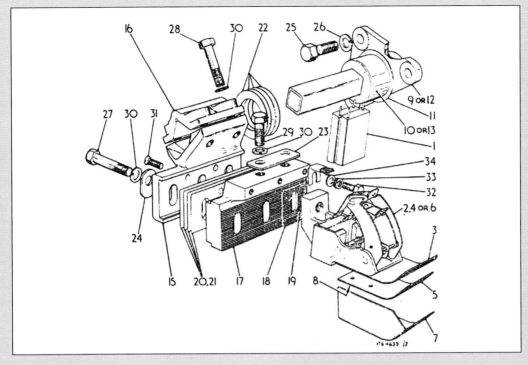

The illustration of one quarter of a very simple generator commutator might help. Electricity passes from the rotating commutator through carbon brushes held in place by brush boxes and wiring, to the electrical terminals on the generator frame.

The Class 50 brush box is a much more complicated device than that illustrated and it needs to overcome some of the laws of physics that complicate the process of generating large amounts of DC electricity and passing it back through a commutator.

The illustration from the English Electric Manual shows all the parts and the important items are 2, 4 or 6, the brush holders. These are spring-loaded to keep the correct pressure between the brush and the rotating commutator. Also, items 3, 5 and 7, the flash guards. These stop electricity from jumping between the commutator and the spring yokes of the brush holder.

The full assembly, in the item illustrated, a part-overhauled unit next to a rather worn one, can be clearly seen. Also, unlike the simple generator shown in the picture there are not four, but 12 brush boxes round the circumference of the EE840/4B. Each holds not one but 12 brushes in three sets of four, so 144 in total. Although called brushes, they do not have bristles; each is a solid piece of carbon

which is wired to the brush box using a piece of copper braid called a pig tail.

Depending on which of the English Electric documents you read, the EE840/4B is continuously rated between 1.25 and 1.5mw (MegaWatts – 1,000,000 watts) with a 10- or 15-minute rating of 3mw. That's enough power to supply a small town! When this much power gets loose it causes quite a lot of damage as some of the illustrations show here.

While putting together a set of brush boxes from 50040's generator to allow it to go into 50049, it became clear that we did not have enough units to complete the job. Consequently I took home all the parts (about 20 sets) we had in store, to sort out what was worth keeping, component recovery from those beyond salvation and overhaul the rest so we had usable stock for the next time. On closer examination, every single one showed evidence of flashover damage; some had been cleaned up or repaired by BR depot staff and the box assembly pressed back into service. But most of the damage showed no evidence of a repair being done at all.

The photos show the power of electricity to melt and in some cases, vaporise metal and melt plastic. For comparison, a good-condition (pre-overhaul) unit is shown next to a damaged one. In photos 1 and 2 the flashover has melted

a hole in the frame of the brush holder (which appears to be made from a copper/aluminium alloy). The force of electrical discharge and the heat of the mutating metal has burnt away a small section of the glass-fibre flash guard too. Both these flashovers occurred to the toe of the brush holder. The box toe area is the most common place for damage, as the commutator (only a few millimetres away, 1.8 to 3.6mm according to the EE manuals) under this part of the box is likely to be quite different to the

BELOW A set of four
Class 50 brushes.
(Joseph Burr)

voltage at the brushes held by the box (hence the need for the flash guard). But I have seen less dramatic damage to the heel part too (see photos 4 and 5 – both looking at the underside of the brush box parts).

On other brush boxes the heat of a flashover current flowing through the brush box has melted some of the plastic parts (see photo 3). In this case the spring yoke used to keep the brush pushed on to the commutator has been distorted such that it will no longer apply an even centralised pressure to the top of the brush – so is now unusable.

The electric arc created in a flashover not only causes the softer metals in the generator to melt, it also allows them to flow and move. In photo 6 the copper has flowed from the copper stagger plate to the rusty steel mounting bracket. But with 3mw of power behind it (even for a fraction of a second) the copper can also boil and spray on to other parts. Photo 7 shows a coating of small copper splatter dots on the insulator used to mount a brush box.

None of these examples went for overhaul or were put back into store. They were mostly beyond our repair capability.

In conclusion, if our set of spares all came from the same generator then it had a very dramatic end to its life. It burnt like a Catherine wheel for no more than a few seconds and then almost certainly fell silent.

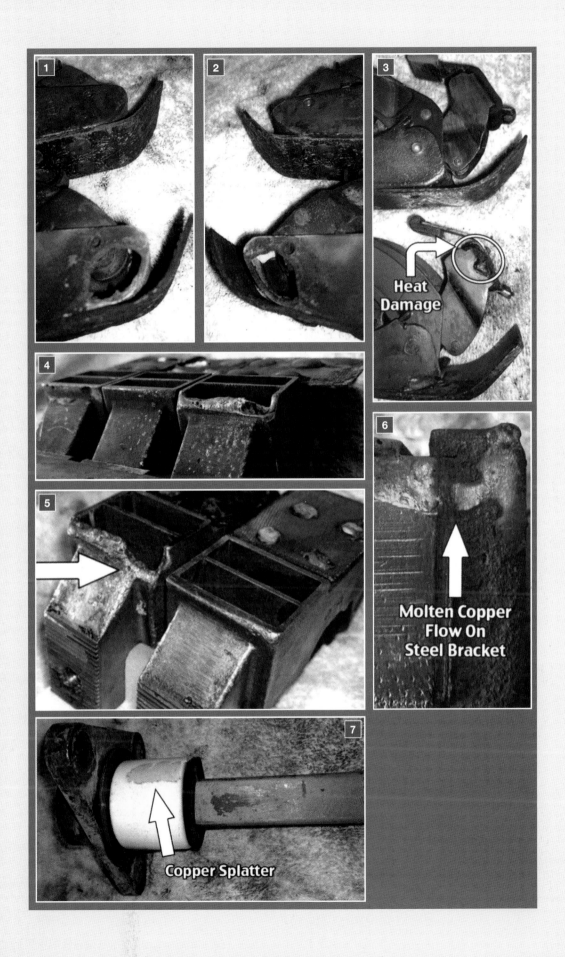

Chapter Five

The owner's view

Class 50s were so popular among enthusiasts that numerous preservation groups were formed to buy locomotives when they were offered for sale by BR. Although 23 made it into preservation, some were not able to be maintained and today, a still tremendously respectable figure of 18 members of the fleet of 50 survive in private ownership. There has even been a return to the main line for several examples.

OPPOSITE Nos. 50049, 50044, 50026, 50017 and 50007 make for an impressive line-up at the Old Oak Common open day on 2 September 2017. *(Tony Middleton)*

The trials and tribulations of restoring a Class 50

During the late 1980s/early 1990s, Class 50s were being rapidly withdrawn. If a loco suffered a generator flashover or major power unit failure it was in trouble. With the drawdown of the fleet having begun any loco suffering such a fault would be seriously considered to be taken out of service and placed in storage pending disposal.

The withdrawn locomotives were placed in sidings, sometimes within Old Oak Common or Laira depots, but others were in locations somewhere quite remote, where they were unprotected from the elements. Many of the withdrawn locomotives also suffered at the hands of vandals and thieves who wrecked the cabs and stole valuable internal equipment, especially generator and traction motor cabling.

At the time, several preservation groups were formed with the intention to buy a Class 50 from British Rail when they were put up for sale by tender. The choice of loco was in many cases assisted by knowing details of its recent history, such as if it had recently received a refurbished main generator, which would offer some reassurance that this should not fail in private hands.

BELOW The condition of a Class 50 at the beginning. This is No. 50029 *Renown* of the Renown Repulse Restoration Group at Peak Rail, Derbyshire. *(Martin Hart)*

ABOVE RIGHT Components stored inside No. 50030 *Repulse*, awaiting restoration. *(Martin Hart)*

RIGHT No. 50030 while under restoration and stored outside. The tarpaulins help to protect the loco from water ingress. *(Martin Hart)*

FAR LEFT A bank of cylinders on The Fifty Fund's No. 50035 *Ark Royal* undergoing restoration.
(Tony Middleton)

LEFT Red oxide painted on to a bank of cylinders during the restoration of No. 50035's engine.
(Tony Middleton)

The bodywork and bogies were also a serious consideration, as large areas of corroded bodywork and heavily worn wheelsets were work to be avoided as much as possible.

Once a loco had been bought and a home for it was secured, it was then important to make arrangements for its swift transfer to the relevant group's care, where prior to beginning the restoration, the first urgent task was to offer protection to prevent any further deterioration, both internally and externally. Most would continue to be stored outside, where tarpaulins to prevent water ingress are a simple and common form of protection.

A thorough inspection of the locomotive was the next task, during which all areas which

ABOVE The final assembly of a restored engine for No. 50035, with gaskets fitted.

LEFT The first Class 50 engine lift in preservation, as carried out on No. 50149 *Defiance*.
(Richard Holmes)

ABOVE Fifty Fund volunteers cleaning up the empty engine room of No. 50035. *(Jon Dunster)*

ABOVE A fully restored and painted engine as fitted into No. 50033 *Glorious*. *(Paul Furtek)*

RIGHT During the restoration of No. 50033 at Laira, for presentation to the National Railway Museum, some areas of corroded bodywork had to be removed and replaced. *(Paul Furtek)*

BELOW With the engine removed the engine room of No. 50026 *Indomitable* has been cleaned to almost new condition. *(Martin Hart)*

FAR LEFT The cab of No. 50030 *Repulse* during strip-down for restoration. *(Martin Hart)*

LEFT The cab of No. 50026 having been stripped for restoration. *(Martin Hart)*

FAR LEFT The control panel of No. 50030 during its rebuild. *(Martin Hart)*

LEFT The restored cab controls of No. 50026. *(Martin Hart)*

LEFT The bodyside of No. 50033 with many areas treated with filler, ready for rubbing down in March 1994. *(Paul Furtek)*

ABOVE No. 50050 *Fearless* during its restoration, returning it to original condition as No. D400 at Laira.

ABOVE RIGHT No. 50033 in undercoat during its repaint at Laira.

RIGHT No. 50023 part-way through repaint into NSE livery.

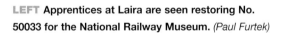

LEFT Apprentices at Laira are seen restoring No. 50033 for the National Railway Museum. *(Paul Furtek)*

BELOW The restored body of No. 50026 awaiting a lift back on to its bogies. *(Martin Hart)*

needed attention were identified. Then the tasks for restoration could be prioritised in a logical order: attention to the power unit, restoration of the electrical systems and testing of them, an overhaul of the braking system, refurbishment of the cabs and attention to the bodywork followed by a complete repaint of the locomotive.

Even if the group was lucky enough to get a loco that had most of the bodywork in relatively sound condition, it would be likely that parts of the roof and areas under the cab windows would need attention as these are common areas for corrosion on the class. Plenty of rubbing down, applying filler and preparation in primer is needed before the top coat of paint can be applied.

LEFT One of the last tasks of a complete Class 50 restoration is to fit the nameplates, as seen here as 50033 regains its *Glorious* name. *(Paul Furtek)*

BELOW The end result! The Fifty Fund's resplendent No. 50044 *Exeter* seen appropriately, on display at the Exeter Rail Fair on 1/2 May 1994.

The Fifty Fund's work

During 1993, The Fifty Fund had No. 50031 Hood operational, out on loan at the Severn Valley Railway, with Nos 50035 Ark Royal and 50044 Exeter based at St Leonards in East Sussex. At the time, work was being concentrated on No. 50044, which was undergoing a cosmetic 'de-refurbishment' programme. The Network SouthEast livery was stripped, new metal was used to replace the corroded areas on the cab sides and also to fill the area where its number had been cut out when the loco was thought to be awaiting the cutter's torch. Sand boxes were refitted and the bodysides prepared with filler used to smooth the surface. A new cut-away roof section was fitted too.

On 28 November 1992, the loco was started for the first time in preservation. However, the seals of one of the cylinder liners had perished, causing water to pass into the sump. To get at the defective seal the cylinder head, piston, con-rod and liner had to be removed. When the liner seals were being replaced it was noted that the bearing shells on the con-rod were worn and needed replacing. This was done while the partial stripdown was carried out, but revealed the other 30 bearing shells would also need early replacement.

The engine was reassembled, some minor electrical work was carried out and the air system charged so that a brake test and sequence test could be made. The engine was started again on 25 July 1993 and was found to be running satisfactorily. The big test was then to see if the loco could move under its own power, which it did successfully.

The bodywork was then rubbed down smooth so that grey primer could be applied ready for a top coat of BR blue. Over the winter the 30 worn bearing shells were replaced.

To give an overview of the work that needs to be carried out for a major overhaul of the cylinder heads let's now turn to a description of the same work as carried out on No. 50035 Ark Royal. This loco had last run on 21 December 1996 on The Fifty Fund's 'Christmas Pudding III' dining train, and the work outlined below was carried out in 1998.

Although No. 50035 had been used on the dining train top-and-tailing with No. 50044, it was shutting down when power was applied above notch 3, and was also suffering from leaking cylinder liners. It was therefore decided to take it out of service, and from January 1997, begin to rectify all the loco's faults which would include the removal of all 16 cylinder heads. The first job was to drain the engine coolant to avoid frost damage over the harsh winter period.

As the work began it was discovered the exhaust valves were heavily coked up with

BELOW Following the rededication of No. 50149, the loco joined Laira's Nos D400 and 50033 for a performance of the 'Laira concerto', conducted by Depot Engineer Malcolm Wishart. Malcolm is seen standing in front of No. D400 as all three locos burst into life. (Paul Furtek)

FAR LEFT No. 50044 *Exeter* made its preservation debut in 'unrefurbished' condition at the Severn Valley Railway diesel gala in 1994.

LEFT An immaculate No. 50015 *Valiant* awaits its departure for Bury on the East Lancashire Railway.

carbon deposits, so it was decided to remove them for attention. All associated inlet manifolds and coolant pipes were removed for cleaning and painting. The engine lubricating oil was drained out in order to allow the sump to be thoroughly cleaned before refilling with fresh oil. At this time there had to be a temporary break in the work while the volunteers turned their attention to No. 50031 *Hood* as it became a priority to have that loco ready for the main line debut of a preserved Class 50.

Once attention returned to No. 50035, the next task was to remove the water rails and inlet manifolds. Then the cylinder heads on B bank were removed starting with B8. Working

from right to left in this way makes it easier to release the water elbows from the cylinder heads as the removals process advances.

With all the heads detached it was then time to unbolt the big end caps and withdraw the pistons. This is a very labour-intensive task, as access is extremely limited through the crankcase door. In addition, the engine has to

BELOW Following a visit to the Mid-Hants Railway, No. 50021 *Rodney* left the railway on a low-loader on the morning of 24 November 1992 for delivery to the Gloucestershire Warwickshire Railway. However, when the tractor unit attempted to turn left into Alresford High Street it became stuck, not arriving at Toddington until 2 December. The police arrived and duly closed the road for four hours while the stranded loco was gradually manoeuvred. *(Paul Furtek)*

ABOVE In March 1994 the recently restored No. 50033 *Glorious* was handed over to the NRM to become part of the National Collection.

rod were withdrawn through the bottom of the liner and the problem was identified as a bent connecting rod.

The bottom of the connecting rod had spread, which had prevented it from being removed through the liner. Problems like this are always a possibility when carrying out this kind of work – there is always something unexpected that can present itself to upset the plans! The damage had been caused by a hydraulic lock while in BR service due to rain water from the exhaust collecting in the cylinder.

To prevent things like this from occurring in Fifty Fund ownership, the volunteers always bar their locomotives' engines by hand to check for hydraulic locking prior to starting the power unit. Fortunately an inspection and measurement of the crankpin for that cylinder showed there was no damage, otherwise it would have been a very costly and time-consuming repair.

All the big end bearing shells removed from B bank were inspected and found to have surface defects. These were replaced during reassembly. With all the liners removed the B bank block was cleaned, sprayed with red oxide and then painted light grey. The same process then followed for A bank.

The cylinder heads were stripped down and the inlet and exhaust ports cleaned to remove

be barred over to reach each bolt in turn – four per big end!

All went well with the removal of pistons B8 to B2. However, while lifting B1 the bottom of the connecting rod jammed in the liner skirt and would not withdraw. Following much deliberation, and a minor dressing of the connecting rod which did not resolve the problem, it was decided to remove the piston, connecting rod and liner as one piece by pushing the liner out using hydraulic jacks supported within the crankcase. The whole assembly was then lifted out of the loco. Once that had been done the piston and connecting

RIGHT *Sir Edward Elgar* was kept in GWR livery in preservation for a number of years, but has now been returned to its BR blue No. 50007 *Hercules* guise.

oil and carbon deposits. The heads were inspected for defects and the valves and valve seats examined for wear and pitting. Twelve heads and their valves required attention, including one with worn valve guides and another with cracks between the valve seats, which had to be stitch-welded to repair.

Meanwhile, the 16 liners were honed to remove the glaze which had been mainly caused by excessive idling in BR times. The pistons were cleaned and new piston rings fitted as required. The cylinder heads were then painted, reassembled and fitted to the power unit. Cleaned and repainted inlet manifold sections and water rails were then put back in place and to complete the work, the sump had new oil filters fitted, and was filled with new oil.

When the engine was reassembled it underwent an extensive bedding-in programme. This required hours of running at idle, and periods at notches 1 to 7. Just after being fired up for the first time the bearing shells were checked and once running, the oil pressure was monitored to make sure it was sufficient for the oil to get through to the bearings.

If the pressure had dropped, serious damage could have resulted. After ten minutes' running the engine was shut down so that further precautionary checks could be made. The series of tests were then carried out with the power unit running for several hours at a time at different settings. After 40 hours of running the fine oil filter was checked for any debris, and fortunately, none was found which was a good sign. Once that was completed the loco was load tested and then passed as fit for a return to service.

Obviously this work is all done on a voluntary basis, except for when components need to be sent away for repair by a specialist company. Therefore, once this amount of work has been invested in a locomotive care is taken not to misuse it with careless driving – especially as in many cases, those driving the locos are the same people who have to fix them! The locomotives have probably never been treated with so much care and precaution as they are now. They are no longer fleet workhorses but are the priceless assets of enthusiasts who wish to share the Class 50 with those who knew it in BR service and with future generations who

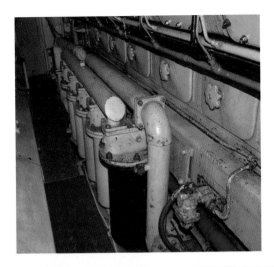

LEFT A set of oil filters attached to the power unit of No. 50035.

BELOW This is what a Class 50 looks like when left abandoned for many years. This is Nos 50001 and 50045 seen while at Booth Roe's Rotherham scrapyard.

ABOVE A view of the poor state of the engine of a long-withdrawn Class 50.

would otherwise never have known the story of this revolutionary machine of the late 1960s.

The first power unit lift in preservation

History was made on 2 July 1994 when Project Defiance, the owning group of No. 50149 *Defiance*, became the first group in preservation to lift a power unit and main generator out of a Class 50. The work was required as earth faults had been detected on the locomotive's first test run when a flashover occurred, and so the engine and main generator would need to be craned out in order to separate the generator and send it for repair.

In BR days, this was a common occurrence and the facilities and equipment were readily

available, but in private hands such a procedure was an unknown undertaking. A mobile 45-tonne crane was hired, which meant that the 30-tonne Class 50 engine was well within its limits. Much preparation work had been carried out prior to the lift, as there are a lot of ancillary components which needed to be disconnected beforehand. A lifting beam had been borrowed.

The lift went smoothly, and once the engine was suspended in mid-air the loco was shunted back and the engine was lowered on to a flat wagon and secured. The main generator was then separated from the engine block with former Laira fitter Mike Woodhouse on hand to assist Project Defiance's Chris Holland and Richard Holmes, who were controlling the proceedings. With the engine removed the opportunity was taken to clean the empty engine room of years of accumulated grime on the walls and deposits of oil and gunge on the floor. Roof panels and lots of pipework that had already been removed had been scrubbed, cleaned and painted, so the cleaning of the engine room would make *Defiance* the cleanest preserved Class 50 at the time.

Meanwhile, the troublesome generator was sent to a specialist firm, Dowding & Mills, for repair. The cause of the earthing faults was tracked down to a pitted patch of the windings just the size of a 5-pence piece! The repaired generator was cleaned and put back together and was hardly recognisable from the unit that had been sent away.

On 16 August the generator was craned back on to the engine. Crankshaft deflection readings were taken to ensure the generator and engine were aligned. Next, the two turbo-blowers, which sit on top of the generator, were refitted along with their corresponding intercoolers. One of the intercoolers was a new one, as traces of leakage were found in the radiator matrix of the old unit.

The engine was returned to the loco on 10 September after once again, much preparatory work. New parts fitted included two rubber engine mounting pads and several associated washers, which had been found to be badly contaminated. After bolting down the engine, the train heating generator was aligned and the crankshaft deflection rechecked, while other volunteers proceeded to refit the many oil and water pipes which had been removed to take the engine out. The engine was started on 24 September, just 18 weeks after the fateful flashover.

This work had been undertaken at the Williton depot of the Diesel & Electric Preservation Group on the West Somerset Railway. On 18 October, No. 50149 made a series of test runs between Crowcombe Heathfield and Bishop's Lydeard with four coaches in tow. All fortunately went well, so *Defiance* was ready for the railway's diesel gala the following weekend.

The work was all made worthwhile when No. 50149 burst through a tape on 28 October 1994 to mark its formal debut run in preservation. It made numerous trips over the diesel gala weekend and performed faultlessly throughout.

The long road home – No. 50031's return to the main line

Jonathan Dunster, former chairman of The Fifty Fund, provides a fascinating insight into the return of No. 50031 to the main line.

"As far as the state of play for our Class 50s was concerned, it was difficult at the end of 1996 to imagine 1997 would be any different from any previous year. We entered the year with both Nos 50031 and 50035 out of service with a large programme of work ahead. However, none of us would ever have predicted that by the end of 1997 a Class 50 would have returned to the main line, and that it would be one of ours!

"Of course, the main talking point at the end of 1996 was the return to the main line of 'Deltic' No. D9000 *Royal Scots Grey*. I, along with many others, stood on Platform 1 at King's Cross on the evening of 2 January 1997 to savour the scene after the arrival of the 'Deltic Reunion' railtour. This was 15 years to the day since the same loco had performed the last rites for the Class 55 in BR service.

"It was without doubt a very poignant moment. One or two people there surprised me by saying how much they hoped that The Fifty Fund would one day be able to return a Class 50 to its rightful 'home' – the main line. Little did I realise that less than eight months later what had seemed nothing more than a pipe dream would become very much a reality.

"In late February, I was at Bewdley attending a meeting with SVR General Manager Alun Rees to discuss the diesel running season. At the end of the meeting, Alun asked me to stay behind as there was another matter he wished to discuss. In his normal direct style, Alun simply asked, 'would you consider main line running with the Class 50s?'

"After recovering from the shock, I replied that although it was probably a dream held by many preserved diesel owners to run on the main line, the amount of work and cost involved had seemed to put this out of reach of most groups. The reason for Alun's enquiry was due to an approach from Andy Staite of Past Time Rail Limited who was seriously interested in using a Class 50 on some of his main line operations.

"As the Severn Valley Railway already had a wide experience of main line operations with the steam fleet, Alun was able to explain in detail what would be required in order to gain the necessary certification. For a vehicle to run over Railtrack metals it had to be examined by an approved Vehicle Acceptance Body (VAB) licensed by Railtrack. Although there were a number of such VABs, the SVR already dealt with Resco for their steam locomotives and support coaches, so they were also approached about the Class 50.

"Before a meeting was arranged with Resco's engineers, we of course had to decide which locomotive would be nominated to make the main line debut for the class. As both Nos 50031 and 50035 were out of service, by default No. D444 became the main line

ABOVE No. 50031 *Hood*'s main line certification meant that it became capable of taking itself and other locomotives away for visits to other railways, such as this scene of it at Minehead on the West Somerset Railway in 1998.

candidate. Prior to the meeting with Resco's engineers we compiled a dossier containing detailed information regarding the condition of the locomotive when purchased with details of all subsequent work carried out by ourselves.

"This information was sent to Resco for their perusal prior to the meeting. At the meeting itself it soon became apparent that registration of the loco would be reasonably straightforward if it passed the main safety examination. Alun Rees had already decided to add our locomotives to the SVR's register of main line certified vehicles and his maintenance policy document, to which a supplement was added to cover the 50s.

"After this first meeting, we invited Resco's certification engineer, Wayne Jones, to have a quick look over the loco prior to undertaking the full safety exam. The condition of the loco was good enough for Wayne to decide there and then it was a going concern and he gave us a copy of the full safety exam for us to carry out ourselves before he returned to do it officially. This allowed us to highlight any problem areas and rectify them before Wayne returned.

"Only two items caused us problems. The AWS (automatic warning system), which of course had not been used since 1990, required some attention to return it to working order. However, the other item was far more serious – the main generator. We discovered the insulation resistance readings were below the minimum acceptable for main line certification, basically due to a build-up of oil and carbon deposits on the windings inside the generator itself.

"Although it did improve marginally after cleaning by hand it was still unacceptable. After consultation with some specialists on large electrical machines it was decided that No. D444 was fit to continue running on the SVR for now, but would definitely need to have major attention to the generator as soon as possible as its condition would only deteriorate to a point where a very expensive failure would occur. Despite this news, No. D444 underwent the full Resco examination on 8 August, which it passed with the exception, of course, of the main generator.

"This left us with a small problem as we were now committed to providing a locomotive for Past Time on 18 October and 1 November. The tours had been advertised, but we didn't have a locomotive! Obviously, the spotlight then fell on No. 50031. At the time in question (early August) this loco was midway through a 12-month maintenance programme which had begun in October 1996.

"Originally, it had been intended to have it ready for traffic in time for the SVR diesel gala in October, so things would have to step up a gear! I have to say at this point that the sheer dedication of our regular volunteers never ceases to amaze me. In order to have No. 50031 ready for the full Resco exam, many days of hard work had to be put in. On 28 August, 50031 underwent the exam and passed, thus becoming the first Class 50 certified to run over Railtrack metals under its own power.

"Passing the engineering exam is not the end of the process, however. There is also the small detail of training drivers. On the fragmented main line railway of the time, all charter trains were operated by English, Welsh & Scottish Railways (EWS). After taking into consideration the proposed routes of the first tours it was decided that Bescot, Acton and Bristol drivers would be

BELOW Main line certificated No. 50031 *Hood* stands at Crewe with an overnight charter to Cardiff and return.

trained. The criteria being that only drivers with previous Class 50 experience would be involved, receiving a one-day refresher course held at the SVR. Two courses were held, the first at the end of September for traction inspectors and the second in early October, for the drivers.

"During September, however, there was an unexpected turn of events. When we entered into the main line project it was well known that other Class 50 owners had the same aim. However, we were as surprised as the next man when a tour was advertised for 4 October using a Class 50! Needless to say, with the fragile nature of the enthusiasts charter market this resulted in confusion as to which would be the first Class 50 tour. The result was that both October tours were cancelled due to a lack of bookings.

"I think it is also fair to say that many people did not believe the stories in the press because No. 50031 had not received any major works attention prior to certification (unlike Pete Waterman's Class 46 No D172 and 'Deltic' No. D9000), and this also contributed to poor bookings. The important fact to note, however, was this. In both cases, Nos D172 and D9000 had stood out of use for some considerable time before being returned to use on the main line. Both Nos 50031 and D444 had been maintained in regular service on the SVR and this, together with our detailed technical records, enabled Resco to consider both locomotives as they stood without the need for any major attention first.

"However, despite all the ill-informed comments it was pleasing to find that bookings for 1 November's 'Pilgrim Hoover' were healthy, and so the scene was set for the return of a Class 50 to their rightful 'home' on the main line. It would be a classic Birmingham to Plymouth and return (taking in a few hills along the way!).

"Although mass hype surrounded the class in their decline with a few tatty examples plodding up and down the Waterloo–Exeter route, this tour would evoke memories of the halcyon days of the mid-1980s when the Class 50s regularly stormed the Lickey on 'Cross-Country' services of 12 or 13 vehicles. At this point it would also be fair to say that most of us closely involved had a few sleepless nights in the week leading up to the event itself. It was without doubt a risky venture to attempt such a challenging route as our maiden run, but we were quietly confident that *Hood* would not let us down.

"Just to be on the safe side however, we had the loco examined by two of my colleagues from Virgin Trains, Dave Yates and Brian Stockton, who both had previous experience of 50s. After a run to Bridgnorth they pronounced it fit, and our thanks are due to them for their time and effort. We also managed to secure the services of Laira's 'Mr Class 50', Mike Woodhouse to accompany the loco on the big day – so we felt we had done all we could and it was now in the lap of the gods.

"At 06.52 on Saturday, 1 November 1997, No. 50031 moved off SVR metals at Kidderminster and on to the national network under her own power and thus made history in the process. We backed on to the stock at Birmingham International at 08.00 and the rest, as they say, is 'history'! Suffice to say, *Hood* proved once and for all to everyone who witnessed the event, just what a fine thoroughbred machine it really is. It was a very proud day for The Fund and all who had worked so hard over the years to make such a memorable occasion possible."

BELOW The main line running of preserved Class 50s brought about the welcome sight of these locos at Penzance once more. Here, Nos 449 and 431 are seen during a refuelling stop at Long Rock depot.

The story of The Fifty Fund, so far...

The Fifty Fund was launched in 1989, when founding shareholder and first Chairman, Dave Keogh, wished to preserve a Class 50. At the time, it seemed unlikely that many of these complex locomotives would be saved, and the original plan has been described as being 'written on the back of a fag packet'.

However, on 20 April 1991, the Fund was in a position to buy No. 50035 *Ark Royal* for £16,500. The loco was formally handed over to Dave Keogh by Network SouthEast Chairman Chris Green at that year's Old Oak Common open day. It was moved to the Fund's first home at St Leonards, East Sussex, in September.

In August of the same year, Fund board members had inspected No. 50044 *Exeter* and subsequently bought that loco in December.

Also, No. 50031 *Hood* was purchased by two shareholders for use by the Fund the same month.

From its outset, The Fifty Fund has been the leading light in Class 50 preservation, and after seeing several of his former charges being sold to them, Laira Fleet Manager Geoff Hudson commented: 'Over the years my respect and sheer admiration of The Fifty Fund has grown and the professionalism of this group can no longer be said to be railway enthusiasts, but professional railway maintainers. They've now done the easy bit, they've maintained and restored the locos. The hard bit, though, is to keep the locos operational and in traffic.

'It may seem glamorous to own Class 50s, but the reality of maintaining them is that it's a long, hard slog requiring an almost bottomless bank balance. I'm sure with their skill and dedication, groups such as The Fifty Fund will keep the locos operational for years to come and people will be able to savour the sight and sound of a pair of 50s at full chat. From all here at Laira we wish them well for the future.'

No. 50031 *Hood* arrived at St Leonards from Laira on 10 March 1992 and was fired up later the same day. At the Fund's AGM on 14 March 1992, all three locomotives were positioned outside for a photo call. No. 50044 had one end painted in original Network SouthEast livery for this occasion only.

One key ingredient to the Fund's long-term success was getting an extensive supply of

spares from the outset. To that end the Fund put a lot of investment into securing whatever Class 50 spares were becoming available as BR continued the rundown of the fleet. This included a spare power unit which came from No. 50018 while members also looked at other sources, such as the final scrapping of No. 50001 at Booth Roe's at Rotherham, which saw a missing major item finally secured – a spare bogie and wheelset.

In May 1992, the Fund operated the first revenue-earning passenger train in preservation when No. 50031 *Hood* had charge of the Bewdley–Kidderminster service on the Severn Valley Railway. Later that year, on 3 August, No. 50035 was fired up for the first time in preservation. The same year a ballot voted to restore No. 50044 *Exeter* to unrefurbished condition as the class had appeared during the late 1970s/early 1980s. By the end of the year, No. 50044 had also been started for its first time in preservation.

In 1993, No. 50031 *Hood* appeared at diesel galas on the Mid-Hants Railway and at the Midland Railway Centre. The following year, *Exeter* made its debut running in unrefurbished condition at the Severn Valley Railway. On 18 September 1996, No. 50035, by then having been repainted in large logo livery, was moved to Kidderminster by road, the SVR having become the Fund's permanent home. It was from there that No. 50031 was made operational for its main line return on 1 November 1997, as described earlier.

The Class 50 Alliance

Many readers will have heard of the Class 50 Alliance (C50A), but may not know exactly what this organisation is. In 2006, The Fifty Fund agreed to merge its ownership and maintenance responsibilities with Project Defiance, the owners of No. 50049 *Defiance*. It was this new, combined organisation, which became known as the Class 50 Alliance. Ownership of Nos 50035, 50044 and 50049 transferred to the Alliance, as did the custodianship of No. 50031.

The Fifty Fund has continued as the public 'face' of the organisation, dedicated to fund-raising, promotion of the Class 50, and selling shares in the Alliance. Class 50 Alliance Ltd

LEFT The Fifty Fund's locos now have a purpose-built diesel servicing shed, complete with pits and lifting equipment, at their disposal on the Severn Valley Railway at Kidderminster. No. 50044 *Exeter* is seen inside, during October 2016.

became responsible for the maintenance and operation of all four locomotives.

In late 2016, the decision was taken to purchase No. 50007 *Hercules* from Neil Boden. This celebrity loco was purchased primarily for main line work and the purchase was funded by a loan from a number of Class 50 Alliance shareholders. The press release for this read: 'The purchase has only been possible thanks to the tremendous generosity of Phil Swallow and a small number of our existing shareholders, who have kindly provided the finance necessary to secure 50007. The C50A has to repay this loan over the next two years, and we're now embarking on a major fund-raising campaign to encourage shareholders old and new to become part-owners in not only *Hercules*, but the rest of the fleet.'

This brings the C50A fleet up to five locomotives, a staggering 10 per cent of the original BR Class 50 fleet!

BELOW The diesel servicing shed at Kidderminster from the outside, with InterCity-liveried No. 50031 *Hood* in the foreground.

Chapter Six

Class 50 names

The entire Class 50 fleet received the names of Royal Navy warships. This chapters tells the story of their namings.

OPPOSITE No. 50033 *Glorious* stands between turns at Salisbury. Note the loco's unique nameplate position, which was done to read 'Glorious Network SouthEast'.

Former Laira fitter Mike Woodhouse describes the naming of the Class 50s in this extract from his 1990 book of memoirs, *Blood, Sweat and Fifties*:

Nameplates ahoy!

"During the summer of 1977 the Western Region management made the decision to name all of the Class 50 fleet. In keeping with the tradition of naming locos with naval connections, the 50s were to be called 'Warships', as had the earlier diesel-hydraulic Classes 41/42/43. Many of the names had previously been carried by LMS steam 'Jubilees'. Although the appellation 'Warships' did not stick, the names themselves have helped greatly to boost the popularity of the Fifties.

"Any enthusiast visiting Laira's loco stores at Christmas 1977 would have had a treat indeed, in the form of seeing 100 gleaming red and silver cast nameplates, fresh from the presses at Swindon. At the time the names had not been assigned to individual locos, and it was my job to label each plate when the decision was made. We had the task of fitting plates not just to our own allocation, but also to the six based at Bristol Bath Road. A few naming ceremonies were planned, but in most cases the plates were fixed without fuss at the depot.

"First to escape from anonymity was 50035. An invitation had been sent to the Navy for the naming of '35 as *Ark Royal*, since it was anticipated that the famous aircraft carrier (based at Plymouth Devonport) would shortly be sailing on her last commission. The previous rail-bound owner of the name had been D601 – also based at Laira, and also one of the depot's favourites. During early January 1978, 50035 came on to the depot for a complete external repaint, cabs included, plus the requisite 'C' exam. I was involved with all this, and with the management we tried to work out the measurements for fitting the nameplates from the drawings that Swindon had sent us.

"It was on 16 January that the first nameplate was actually attached. It was no easy task. The main problem was how to trace up the height and centre of the body. We measured other 50s but they were all slightly different. Eventually a template was made up square to the engine room roof bodyline. With a plate on each side any fitting that was not straight or square would be noticed at a glance. A further difficulty was the variation in plate length, from *Indomitable* (50026) to *Lion* (50027). In the end, a centre tap hole was drilled, adjustments being made with the one bolt before final fixing. A final touch was to remove the oval English Electric Leasings Company plates, if the loco still carried them.

"I must admit that seeing 50035 *Ark Royal* for the first time created a new impression on me: from now on it would have a character of its own. A further distinction was the fitting of white headcode panel lamps. The naming ceremony was performed the next day by Captain Anson of HMS *Ark Royal* at Plymouth North Road station. I believe that today's *Ark* carries in its mess room a nameplate from D601 and a crest from 50035.

"From then on I was involved with the naming of all but the last two of the class to be treated – but more about those later. In the meantime the other 98 plates lay gathering dust in a corner of the stores, as two full months elapsed before the next namings took place. This came about due to a request from RPPR Railtours for two 'namers' for their 'Derby Double' tour on 18 March. At the same time HMS *Dauntless*, the shore establishment near Reading, expressed an interest in a naming ceremony. This tied in well, since 50048, the loco booked for the name *Dauntless*, was due for an 'E' exam and full repaint, 50010 was also on the maintenance exam programme so this too would receive its name, *Monarch*.

"The pair duly emerged from Laira in the early hours of the 16th resplendent with their new names. Both headed east, light engine to Old Oak, '48 later going to Reading for its naming ceremony. 50035 plus 50048 were booked for the double-header from Paddington to Derby, with 50010 as standby; but in the event, *Ark Royal* refused to operate in multiple with *Dauntless* and so '48 and '10 worked the train.

"From this date onwards I would take a note of each Class 50 coming on for repair at Laira and then go and ask the Chief Mechanical Engineer if he would agree to the nameplates being fitted. Of course, some locos were in Doncaster Works at this period, and the Bristol six (50039-044) were hard to remove

from traffic. Sometimes it would only be one, sometimes two, but on 6 April no less than three 'Warships' were named: 50018 as *Resolution*, 50034 *Furious*, and 50007 *Hercules* – a loco later to be surrounded by controversy over its name.

"As it turned out, April 1978 saw the naming on no less than 16 of the class: from then on it became a steady flow. Only after 20 had been done did we get our hands on the first of the Bath Road allocation, when on 26 April, 50044 became *Exeter*. May was also a busy month, the namings tally moving on to 33, the last being 50014 *Warspite* on the 30th. This name had last been carried by 'Jubilee' class 4-6-0 No. 45724.

"By mid-summer only a few were left unnamed. On 4 August ex-D400, now No. 50050, became *Fearless,* but at the last moment the Navy decided to have a naming ceremony, and so the plates were removed on the 7th and put back in the stores. Finally, a suitable date for the ceremony was arranged, and on the afternoon of the 23rd 50050 was officially twinned with its naval namesake, the formalities taking place at the depot itself.

"From then on the flow of namings became a trickle. No more were done in August, but on 1 September my own 50008 acquired the name *Thunderer*. Six were left without names; of these, two were away at Doncaster Works, and two were Bath Road based. These two were caught first; 50040 arriving for tyre turning on 15 September and becoming *Leviathan*, with 50042 receiving its *Triumph* plates some three weeks later.

"My final loco was 50029, which on 14 November, emerged as *Renown*. The other two were still on 'The Plant' at Doncaster, 50006 as the prototype for refurbishment, and 50011 undergoing classified repair. No. 50011 was outshopped in April 1979 with a new power unit, but without any treatment to the bodyside, which was very rough. It ran around in service until being made *Centurion* on 20 August 1979. Meanwhile, the *Neptune* plates for '06 had transferred north to Donny on 20 June. It was the only Fifty to be named on the Eastern Region, finally entering traffic as *Neptune* on 15 December 1979 – last to be named, and also the only unrefurbished class member not to receive a name. Ironically, these two locos were last to be named but first to be withdrawn."

Loco	Name	Date Named	Date Plaque fitted
50001	*Dreadnought*	10.04.1978	-
50002	*Superb*	21.03.1978	12.11.1980
50003	*Temeraire*	09.05.1978	-
50004	*St Vincent*	09.05.1978	09.09.1988
50005	*Collingwood*	05.04.1978	21.11.1987
50006	*Neptune*	25.09.1979	-
50007	*Hercules*[1]	06.04.1978	25.02.1984
50008	*Thunderer*	01.09.1978	20.09.1979
50009	*Conqueror*	08.05.1978	-
50010	*Monarch*	16.03.1978	-
50011	*Centurion*	01.09.1979	15.05.1986
50012	*Benbow*	03.04.1978	-
50013	*Agincourt*	19.04.1978	-
50014	*Warspite*	30.05.1978	-
50015	*Valiant*	21.04.1978	-
50016	*Barham*	03.04.1978	-
50017	*Royal Oak*	24.04.1978	-
50018	*Resolution*	06.04.1978	-
50019	*Ramillies*	18.04.1978	-
50020	*Revenge*	07.07.1978	-
50021	*Rodney*	31.07.1978	-
50022	*Anson*	20.04.1978	-
50023	*Howe*	17.05.1978	-
50024	*Vanguard*	15.05.1978	-
50025	*Invincible*	06.06.1978	07.05.1981
50026	*Indomitable*	29.03.1978	-
50027	*Lion*	17.04.1978	-
50028	*Tiger*	10.05.1978	-
50029	*Renown*	26.10.1978	-
50030	*Repulse*	10.04.1978	-
50031	*Hood*	28.06.1978	22.04.1983
50032	*Courageous*	17.07.1978	11.10.1986
50033	*Glorious*	26.06.1978	-
50034	*Furious*	06.04.1978	-
50035	*Ark Royal*	17.01.1978	17.01.1978
50036	*Victorious*	16.05.1978	-
50037	*Illustrious*	08.06.1978	27.05.1982
50038	*Formidable*	05.05.1978	-
50039	*Implacable*	20.06.1978	-
50040	*Leviathan*[2]	15.09.1978	-
50041	*Bulwark*	08.05.1978	-
50042	*Triumph*	04.10.1978	-
50043	*Eagle*	28.06.1978	-
50044	*Exeter*	27.04.1978	20.08.1981
50045	*Achilles*	12.04.1978	-
50046	*Ajax*	11.10.1978	07.04.1985
50047	*Swiftsure*	26.05.1978	-
50048	*Dauntless*	16.03.1978	-
50049	*Defiance*	02.05.1978	17.07.1988
50050	*Fearless*	23.08.1978	23.08.1978

[1] Renamed *Sir Edward Elgar* on 25.02.1984.

[2] Renamed *Centurion* 07.87 after withdrawal of 50011.

Class 50 numbers

Original No.	To BR	TOPS Renumbered	TOPS No.
D400	03/10/1967	27/02/1974	50050
D401	06/12/1967	21/03/1974	50001
D402	22/12/1967	23/04/1974	50002
D403	15/01/1968	15/02/1974	50003
D404	22/12/1967	02/02/1974	50004
D405	12/01/1968	26/08/1974	50005
D406	23/01/1968	04/03/1974	50006
D407	12/03/1968	12/04/1974	50007
D408	06/02/1968	18/02/1974	50008
D409	06/02/1968	07/01/1974	50009
D410	21/02/1968	07/03/1974	50010
D411	19/03/1968	07/02/1974	50011
D412	28/02/1968	01/02/1974	50012
D413	06/03/1968	19/06/1974	50013
D414	24/04/1968	11/04/1974	50014
D415	02/04/1968	16/03/1973	50015
D416	24/04/1968	13/12/1973	50016
D417	02/04/1968	01/02/1974	50017
D418	11/04/1968	21/03/1974	50018
D419	23/04/1968	13/12/1973	50019
D420	29/04/1968	17/02/1974	50020
D421	01/05/1968	23/11/1973	50021
D422	07/05/1968	15/02/1974	50022
D423	08/05/1968	18/12/1973	50023
D424	21/05/1968	08/05/1974	50024

Original No.	To BR	TOPS Renumbered	TOPS No.
D425	31/05/1968	22/01/1974	50025
D426	12/06/1968	29/07/1973	50026
D427	10/06/1968	08/01/1974	50027
D428	18/06/1968	17/02/1974	50028
D429	21/06/1968	03/03/1974	50029
D430	25/06/1968	18/03/1974	50030
D431	01/07/1968	19/03/1974	50031
D432	12/07/1968	25/02/1974	50032
D433	19/07/1968	23/04/1974	50033
D434	24/07/1968	22/03/1974	50034
D435	30/07/1968	01/03/1974	50035
D436	12/08/1968	28/10/1973	50036
D437	20/09/1968	07/03/1974	50037
D438	16/09/1968	19/02/1974	50038
D439	09/09/1968	27/02/1974	50039
D440	25/09/1968	01/02/1974	50040
D441	03/10/1968	01/03/1974	50041
D442	30/09/1968	01/12/1973	50042
D443	04/10/1968	12/03/1974	50043
D444	11/10/1968	14/02/1974	50044
D445	18/10/1968	21/03/1974	50045
D446	29/10/1968	01/02/1974	50046
D447	05/11/1968	17/02/1974	50047
D448	18/11/1968	08/03/1974	50048
D449	11/12/1968	29/01/1974	50049

Class 50 refurbishments

No.	Date on works	Date work commenced	Date returned to traffic	No.	Date on works	Date work commenced	Date returned to traffic
50006	29.9.77	21.2.78	13.11.79	50016	10.8.81	14.8.81	16.1.82
50003	21.2.79	21.3.79	17.9.80	50009	12.9.81	15.9.81	1.2.82
50017	21.6.79	26.7.79	5.2.80	50037	30.10.81	4.11.81	6.4.82
50019	27.7.79	14.9.79	31.3.80	50021	9.11.81	13.11.81	5.4.82
50001	29.11.79	30.11.79	9.4.80	50044	19.11.81	25.11.81	29.4.82
50047	13.12.79	16.12.79	12.5.80	50042	6.1.82	11.1.82	22.5.82
50013	7.1.80	21.1.80	7.6.80	50029	11.1.82	14.1.82	4.6.82
50023	9.4.80	11.4.80	10.8.80	50025	3.2.82	8.2.82	2.8.82
50038	25.4.80	2.6.80	12.11.80	50005	2.3.82	4.3.82	13.8.82
50004	2.5.80	8.5.80	29.10.80	50048	5.3.82	23.3.82	2.9.82
50022	28.5.80	11.6.80	19.12.80	50028	29.3.82	2.4.82	20.10.82
50032	15.8.80	18.8.80	31.11.80	50034	27.5.82	31.5.82	25.10.82
50015	11.9.80	17.9.80	11.2.81	50024	8.6.82	10.6.82	15.11.82
50020	14.10.80	15.10.80	6.3.81	50026	2.7.82	2.8.82	6.12.82
50035	5.11.80	20.11.80	27.3.81	50018	6.8.82	12.8.82	20.12.82
50012	5.11.80	20.11.80	5.5.81	50007	13.9.82	16.9.82	28.2.83
50010	7.1.81	8.1.81	22.5.81	50046	11.10.82	4.11.82	19.3.83
50036	2.2.81	9.2.81	18.6.81	50011	22.11.82	26.11.82	15.4.83
50040	24.2.81	25.2.81	18.7.81	50043	6.12.82	8.12.82	4.5.83
50045	19.3.81	20.3.81	24.8.81	50049	11.1.83	17.1.83	28.5.83
50039	15.4.81	15.4.81	14.9.81	50050	17.1.83	26.1.83	5.7.83
50033	29.4.81	11.5.81	12.10.81	50027	7.2.83	2.3.83	23.7.83
50041	29.5.81	1.6.81	29.10.81	50030	31.3.83	11.4.83	14.9.83
50031	4.6.81	11.6.81	13.11.81	50002	31.3.83	25.4.83	20.10.83
50008	6.7.81	10.7.81	21.12.81	50014	23.5.83	26.5.83	7.12.83

Class 50 liveries

As all Class 50s carried the standard BR Rail blue livery from new, this is not included in the list below, which details subsequent repaints.

Key:

A – Large logo BR blue

B – BR blue with grey roof

C – BR blue with black roof

D – Special livery

E – Original NSE (blue, red, white and light grey)

F – Revised NSE (light blue)

G – Revised NSE (dark blue)

50001	A, B, F		50026	A, B, E
50002	A, B, C, E, G		50027	A, B, C, F, G
50003	A, B, C, F		50028	A, B, C, F
50004	A, B		50029	A, B, E, F, G
50005	A, B, G		50030	A, B, F
50006	A, B, C		50031	A, B
50007	A, B, D		50032	A, B, E
50008	A, B, C, D		50033	A, B, G
50009	A, B, G		50034	A, B, E, G
50010	A, B, C, D		50035	A, B, E, G
50011	A, B, C		50036	A, B
50012	A, B		50037	A, B, D, E, G
50013	A, B		50038	A, B
50014	A, B, C		50039	A, B
50015	A, B, D		50040	A, B
50016	A, B, G		50041	A, B, F
50017	A, B, D, E, G		50042	A, B, C
50018	A, B, E, F		50043	A, B, C, F, G
50019	A, B, D, E		50044	A, B, C, D, E, G
50020	A, B		50045	A, B, G
50021	A, B		50046	A, B, C
50022	A, B		50047	A, B, C
50023	A, B, E, G		50048	A, B, E, G
50024	A, B, C, F, G		50049	A, B, C, D, F
50025	A, B, E		50050	A, B, D, F

BELOW All Class 50s wore standard BR Rail blue from delivery and they were in fact the first class to be delivered from new in that livery. This is No. 50025 *Invincible* at Penzance.

BELOW A resplendent No. 50033 *Glorious* at Laira in large logo BR blue. *(Paul Furtek)*

ABOVE The grey roof of the large logo blue livery quickly became very dirty, so Laira applied black roofs to many locos to mask this.

ABOVE A unique livery was that of No. 50010 *Monarch* in large logo with a blue roof.

ABOVE Original Network SouthEast livery is seen here worn by No. 50034 *Furious*.

BELOW The darker-blue revised Network SouthEast livery as carried by No. 50048 *Dauntless*. Instead of BR double arrows the livery included the NSE 'West of England' brand badge.

ABOVE The first variant of revised Network SouthEast livery, as applied to No. 50050 *Fearless*.

BELOW No. 50007 *Sir Edward Elgar* became a celebrity after receiving its GWR lined-green livery from 1984.

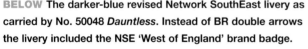

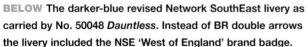

ABOVE No. 50149 *Defiance* was the only Class 50 which received Railfreight General livery in service, during its freight trial work in Cornwall and Devon.

ABOVE A different, larger style of NSE headcode badge as worn by No. 50024 *Vanguard*.

ABOVE No. 50015 *Valiant* was the only Class 50 to wear Civil Engineers' 'Dutch' livery grey and yellow. It had red-backed nameplates on all but its last train, for which it was given more accurate black-backed plates.

BELOW Another loco well-known for its Departmental blue livery was No. 50019 *Ramillies*, although it carried larger numbers than applied to No. 50008.

ABOVE Departmental 'Laira Blue' livery was applied to No. 50008 *Thunderer*, seen here at an open day at Coalville.

BELOW Less well-known for its wearing of Departmental 'Laira Blue' livery was No. 50037 *Illustrious*, which only had this livery for a few weeks. Pictures of it in this guise are very rare.

LEFT No. 50017 wears a non-standard LMS maroon from its VSOE working days.
(Phil Scott)

BELOW D444 wearing a 'might-have-been' BR green livery.
(Hugh Llewelyn)

LEFT No. 50135 Ark Royal in its Load Haul livery offering a new freight take on the 50149 story.
(Tony Hisgett)

Locomotive data and equipment

From BR document 33003/1B

November 1967

English Electric Co Ltd diesel-electric locomotives Nos D400–D449

Type	4
Wheel arrangement	Co-Co
Weight in running order	117 tons
Tractive effort:	
Maximum	48,500lb
Continuous	33,000lb
Wheelbase	56ft 2in
Bogie wheelbase	13ft 6in
Driving wheel diameter (new)	3ft 7in
Bogie centres	42ft 8in
Width overall	8ft 10⅜in
Length overall	68ft 6in
Height overall	12ft 9¹/₁₆in
Minimum curve negotiable	4 chains
Maximum service speed	100mph
Fuel tank capacity	1,100 gals
Lubricating oil capacity:	
Engine sump, lubricating oil cooler, piping etc.	130 gals
Cooling water capacity including charge coolers, etc	Total 305 gals
	200 gals jacket and radiator
	80 gals charge cooler and radiator
	25 gals header tank
Brakes	Compressed air rheostatic and handbrakes on the locomotive, vacuum and air brake equipment giving proportional air/rheostatic braking on the locomotive.

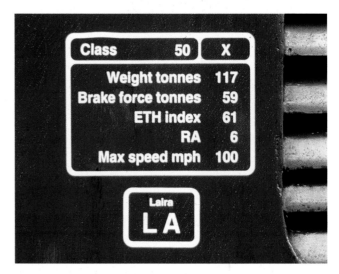

ABOVE A Class 50 data panel.

Power equipment

16-cylinder diesel engine	English Electric Vee-type producing 2,700hp at 850rpm
Direction of rotation: (Looking on the free end of the engine)	Anti-clockwise
Cylinder bore and stroke	10in x 12in
Firing order 'B' bank	1, 5, 7, 3, 8, 4, 2, 6
'A' bank	8, 4, 2, 6, 1, 5, 7, 3
Note: 'A' bank is on the left-hand side when facing the free end of the engine. Cylinders are numbered from the free end.	
Main generator	EE Co
Heating generator	EE Co
Auxiliary generator	EE Co
Traction motors (6)	EE Co
Traction motor gear ratio	5³/₁₈, i.e. 53 teeth on the axle pinion and 18 teeth on the traction motor pinion giving a reduction of 2.9:1.

Auxiliary equipment with which drivers may be concerned when carrying out their duties

Component	Location
Traction motor blowers (2)	No. 1 blower in clean air compartment (in rear of radiators).
	No. 2 blower in equipment compartment immediately in front of No. 2 cab, 'B' bank side.
Radiator fan (electrically driven from train heating generator)	In roof between radiator banks.
Air compressors (2)	Under-floor-mounted on either side of locomotive, ahead of the fuel tank.
Vacuum exhausters (2)	No. 1 exhauster on 'A' bank side below brake equipment frame.
	No. 2 exhauster on 'B' bank side below No. 2 traction motor blower.
Pressurising fan (electrically driven from train heating generator)	In roof above train heating and auxiliary generators.
Rheostatic brake fans (2) (driven by traction motors during rheostatic braking)	On 'A' bank side of gangway opposite electrical cubicle.
Fuel transfer pump	On clean-air compartment bulkhead in engine room 'B' bank side.
Dust extraction fan	In clean-air compartment 'B' bank side on floor.
Battery – lead acid 110 volts.	In boxes under-floor-mounted on 'A' and 'B' bank sides in rear of fuel tank.

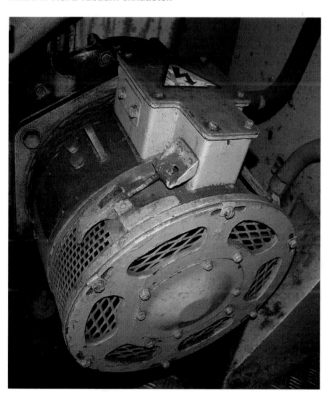

BELOW No. 2 vacuum exhauster.

BELOW Selector switches for different modes of operation. Left to right: vacuum exhauster, brake system, and compressor.

AWS and DSD operation and braking system

The Automatic Warning System (AWS) and Driver's Safety Device (DSD) system are supplied with air at 100lb/in^2 through a limiting valve. This supplies the standard air-operated AWS equipment at each cab end (the change-end switches are behind the driver's seat in each cab), and the brake application unit (to left of the Westinghouse frame).

In the cab in which the driver is working, with the change-end switch at 'On', air passes direct to the EP valve, but not beyond the change-end switch. The AWS reservoirs are fed through the EP valve. The AWS pipe is fed through an internal choke in the brake application unit (port 4 to port 2).

An AWS application occurs when the EP valve is de-energised. This connects the supply air to the horn (through a choke) and exhausts the reservoir to atmosphere (through another choke). Thus the pressure in the AWS pipes falls during a delay period. This operates the brake feed cut-off valve (to prevent the normal flow of air through the auto-air-valve to the air brake pipe) and is sensed by the AWS application unit, which reduces the air-brake pipe pressure, to apply the locomotive and train brakes.

Cancellation of the AWS warning re-energises the EP valve, which stops the horn blowing and seals off the AWS reservoir to allow it to be recharged through the brake application unit and AWS pipe.

When the change-end switch is placed in the 'Off' position (or the emergency handle is turned to 'Isolate') there is an air feed through to the EP valve which is held in the 'Energised' position by air pressure.

BELOW A schematic diagram of the AWS and DSD air equipment. *(British Rail)*

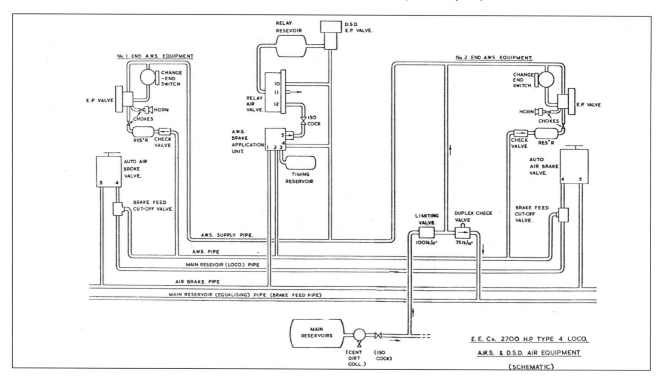

Normally, the DSDEP valve is energised and the relay reservoir charged with air. If the driver's pedal is not kept in the 'balanced' position (and the vigilance sequence maintained) the DSDEP valve is de-energised. This commences to exhaust the relay reservoir. When the pressure in this has fallen from $100lb/in^2$ to $50lb/in^2$ (the five to seven seconds delay period), the relay air valve vents port 5 of the brake application unit, which then drops the AWS pipe pressure. The brake application takes place in the same manner as for an AWS application.

(The relay air valve, relay reservoir and DSDEP valve are all above and in rear of the brake application unit.)

An isolating cock is provided (to the rear of the fire bottle tops) to blank off the relay air valve from the brake application unit, if there is a failure of the DSD equipment. Closing this cock prevents a DSD application being made.

NOTE: If main supply reservoir pressure falls below $95lb/in^2$ the brake application unit vents the AWS pipe until main reservoir pressure has been reached, or is restored to $95lb/in^2$. This provides a safeguard against moving, or continuing to move, the locomotive without sufficient reserve of air to operate the brakes.

Vacuum-brake defects – procedure

When a test is to be made in connection with a vacuum brake defect, the following procedure is to be adopted.

Vacuum-brake efficiency test

It is important that the diesel engine MUST be running to operate the exhausters for this test.

Place the brake selector switch to 'Vacuum braked' position.

Take the vacuum hose at No. 1 end off the dummy coupling and move driver's auto brake valve to 'Release' position, watch the vacuum gauge and if more than 3in of vacuum is obtained it is an indication that there is a stoppage in the apparatus which must be located and removed. Replace pipe at No. 1 end and repeat operation at No. 2 end. Create 21in of vacuum and stop the engine. Note the time taken for vacuum to fall to 12in in the train pipes. If this is less than 30 seconds, it is an indication that undue leakage is occurring and this must be found.

Restart the engine and with the auto air-brake valve in 'Running' position:

Take the hose pipe off the dummy coupling at one end of the locomotive and place the special disc with a $\frac{3}{16}$in diameter leak hole in the end of the hose pipe. Ascertain whether 21in of vacuum can be created and maintained with auto air-brake valve in 'Running' position.

NOTE: The brake test should be carried out from each driving cab.

Isolating cocks and release valves

A summary of the cocks provided on the locomotive is given below. Most of these have been referred to in the description of the operation of the equipment.

Bogie brake isolating cocks (4)

These are positioned under the locomotive main frame, two over each bogie, one at each end protecting the flexible air connection from the straight air-brake system to the brake cylinders, and one at each end protecting the flexible connection from the auto air-brake. There is one on either side of the locomotive in the rear of the second axle of the leading bogie, and one on each side forward of the second axle of the trailing bogie.

In the event of failure of a flexible connection, or air-brake on any bogie equipment, the relevant cock(s) should be closed as an emergency measure. Brake power will then not be available to that bogie from the system(s) which has (have) been isolated.

Buffer beam isolating cocks – vented (10)

Shut-off cocks are provided on each buffer beam for the two main reservoir equalising pipes (brake feed pipes) – just inside each buffer, and for the air-brake pipe – towards the centre of the buffer beam. Close to the equalising pipe cock on each side is a smaller cock for the engine throttle control pipe.

Each of these cocks should be open when the pipes are coupled to another locomotive or vehicle, and shut off before disconnecting.

Main reservoir isolating cock

This seals off the compressors and main reservoirs from the remainder of the system. It is close to the LH rear main reservoir. In the event of fracture or leakage from the compressor/ reservoir system, the locomotive could then be worked from a coupled locomotive if a main supply were available.

Compressor governor isolating cock (vented)

This will be found on 'A' bank side of the auxiliary generator. In the event of the compressor governor not cutting in, the isolating cock can be closed when the compressor(s) will run continuously. Reliance is then placed on the safety valve to control the reservoir pressure.

Distributor air feed isolating cock (sealed)

This shuts off the air supply (via the various EP valves and/or chokes) to the distributor. The automatic brake on the locomotive will be inoperative if this cock is closed. It is on the RH side of the Westinghouse frame (with its associated air strainer).

Restricted application control valve isolating cock (vented)

This is near the base of the fire extinguisher bottles by No. 1 exhauster motor. Closing this cock will render the restricted application control valve ineffective (the release valve above the capacity reservoir – against the bodyside behind the control cubicle) should also be blown down. With this portion of the system isolated, no reduction in brake cylinder pressure will be made to compensate for dynamic braking.

Vacuum isolating cock

If the locomotive is to be hauled dead (without air pressure) in a vacuum-fitted train, this cock (underneath and to the left of the VAI control valve on the Westinghouse frame) is closed. This seals the vacuum brake pipe and the locomotive becomes a piped (but not fitted) vehicle.

DSD isolating cock

In the event of failure of the DSD equipment, this cock can be closed to prevent DSD brake applications (providing a secondman is available to ride with the driver). It is found to the left of the Westinghouse frame level with the fire bottle tops.

AWS isolating cocks (2)

These are incorporated in the usual AWS control boxes which are behind each driver's seat, at floor level. The red handle is moved to 'Isolate' to render the AWS system inoperative.

Radiator shutter air motors isolating cock (vented)

This requires closure to release air pressure on the air motors should the shutters have to be opened manually using the over-riding lever, in an emergency. The cock is in the radiator fan compartment on the 'B' bank side of the air motors.

Horn and windscreen wiper/washer isolating cocks (4)

There are two at each cab end, one feeding the horns and the other the windscreen wipers and washers. They can be found in the bottom of the compartment to the right of the cooker/hot plate. The horn cock is to the left and slightly behind the cock for the windscreen equipment.

Vacuum chamber release valves (2)

There is one in each locomotive cab, on the right-hand side of the desk in front of the assistant's seat. Following vacuum-brake operation and before commencing air-brake operation, one of these valve buttons should be depressed until the vacuum chamber gauge reads zero. The vacuum portion of the distributor will then be inoperative and the locomotive ready for air-brake operation.

Distributor control reservoir release valve

Should it be impossible to fully release the automatic brake on the locomotive, opening this valve will assist the distributor in doing so. It is close to its associated reservoir, mounted under the roof over the Westinghouse frame.

Reference reservoir release valve

If the Restricted Application Control Valve Isolating Cock has to be closed this release valve (above the capacity reservoir behind the control cubicle on the right-hand bodyside) should also be blown down.

Appendix 6

Electronic equipment

Diesel-electric locomotive D400 – November 1969

Generator field regulator

Basic operation

The regulator controls the output of the generator by varying the mean field current over a wide range in response to small DC input signals.

When the switch is closed, current will flow in the generator field, the rate of increase in current being controlled by the inductance of the winding. When the switch is opened, current continues to flow in the winding via the free wheel diode 'D'. The rate of decay in current is also controlled by the inductance of the winding.

If switch 'S' is made to operate at a certain frequency such that the switch is open for a longer period than it is closed, then the mean current in the winding will be small.

The ratio of the period the switch is closed to the period open is called the mark/space ratio and the above diagram represents a small mark/space ratio. If the mark/space ratio is increased so that the switch is closed longer than it is open, then the mean current would increase to a higher value. By varying the mark/space ratio of the switch, the generator field current can be controlled over a wide range. The frequency of operation is chosen so that the ripple current produced by the circuit is negligible. With the KV10 regulator an electronic switch is used incorporating thyristors and the mark/space ratio is varied by an electronic control circuit.

Power circuit – forced commutation

The first gating pulse is applied to the commutating thyristor SCR2 to switch it on. Current flows via the generator field winding to charge the commutating capacitor; the path of the current is A – B – C – D – E. When the capacitor is almost fully charged, the charging current is reduced to a value less than the holding current of SCR2, which then switches off. Although this charging current passes through the generator field winding its effect on the generator output is negligible.

A gating pulse is then applied to the main thyristor SCR1 and current starts to flow in the main field winding. The firing of this SCR completes a series reasonant circuit B – E – D – F – G – C. The commutating capacitor quickly discharges, and due to the inductance of 'L', changes in the reverse direction. Diode D9 prevents further oscillation of the circuit and therefore point 'C' remains at approximately 110V with respect to point 'B'.

When the next gating pulse is applied to SCR2, the commutator capacitor voltage is connected directly across SCR1 which momentarily opposes the current flow and SCR1 is switched off. Also, the commutating capacitor recharges again and the above sequence of events is repeated at 30 IPS.

The above method of control is called forced commutation.

Input units for static load regulator

The basic load regulator gives minimum field current for an input voltage of 44V relative to N, and maximum field current for an input voltage of 22V. The output current is, therefore, inversely proportional to input voltage signal.

An input unit is always used to convert the available signals to a suitable value to operate the load regulator. There are three types of input units commonly used on locomotives:

Input unit NPE7-A9 (NPE7-A1)

This input unit enables the load regulator to be operated directly from a potentiometer connected to a governor vane motor, or from a control system.

The input voltage signal required for this unit is 7V to 37V, 7V giving minimum field current and 37V giving maximum. These signals are inverted by transistor T1 to give output signals of 44V and 22V respectively. Zener diode ZD1 and VR1 provide the bias for T1. Capacitors C1 and C2 control the rate of change of output voltage and ZD2 is included for spike voltage suppression. Components C3, VR3, R4 and D1 form a circuit designed to limit the maximum field current to 140A. This circuit is not now used as it was thought to be introducing voltage spikes into the control circuit.

Operation of input unit NPE7-A2

This unit controls the KV10 field supply unit in response to signals obtained from the engine governor via switches VRS and VLS. The KV10 requires a DC signal between 22 and 44V to control the field, a signal of 44V giving minimum field. The output voltage of the unit from terminal 11 is connected to the KV10 and depends on the charge on capacitor C1.

Transistors T5 and T6 are connected as a double emitter follower. A characteristic of the configuration is a very high input resistance. This is necessary to prevent C1 from discharging via the output circuit. Also, the double emitter follower has a voltage gain of slightly less than one; therefore, the voltage between terminals 8 and 11 is practically the same as the voltage across C1.

When the governor contact VRS closes, R3 and R9 form a potential divider and the base of PNP transistor T4 becomes negative with respect to its emitter and therefore, conducts. When T4 conducts, its collector becomes more positive and therefore, the base of NPN transistor T3 becomes positive with respect to its emitter and also conduces.

This allows a small current to flow via R7 and T3 to charge C1. As C1 is a large value capacitor, the voltage increase on C1 is fairly slow and progressive. Because C1 is connected to the 44V supply an increase in voltage on the capacitor represents a REDUCTION in output voltage on terminal 11 and therefore, the KV10 increases the field current. When the engine is fully loaded, VRS will open and T4 and T3 revert to their non-conducting stage with the voltage across C1 remaining at whatever value it has increased to.

If the engine becomes overloaded VLS operates to turn on T2 and C1 discharges at the same rate through T2 and R2. The resultant increase in voltage at terminal 11, signals the KV10 to turn down the generator field current.

Terminal 14 is connected to transistor T1 which is similar in operation to the above, except that in this case the discharge resistor, R6 is smaller than R2 and therefore, discharges C1 more quickly to turn the field down. The circuit operates when wheelslip occurs and also via motor interlocks when the master handle is in the 'Off' position.

Control unit NPE7-A6

This control unit is used to convert a load regulator into an automatic voltage regulator, and is used to control the train-heat generator.

A signal proportional to train-heat voltage is fed into the control unit through resistor Z23. This is compared with a reference signal provided by R7 and R8. The difference between these two signals called the error signal is fed into the integrating amplifier CA4. When the train-heat voltage is low, the error signal will be negative and this will cause the amplifier output to increase. The amplifier output is connected to the KV10 by an inverting amplifier T2. The positive error signal, therefore, results in an increase in field excitation. When the generator output voltage has increased to the correct value, the error signal disappears and the output of the integrating amplifier remains at the value reached. This is an important characteristic of an integrating amplifier.

If the train-heat voltage is too high, the error signal will be positive and the output voltage of the integrating amplifier will be reduced, giving a reduction in field excitation.

The generator output voltage level may be adjusted by resistor R8.

The bias on transistor T1 is adjusted by resistor R12 so that in the event of an earth fault occurring, the train-heat voltage is reduced by 50V. This is due to all or part of the earth fault current flowing through resistor Z66 and causing transistor T1 to conduct more heavily.

There is some interaction between resistors R8 and R12 and careful adjustments are required to obtain the correct settings. Resistor R3 controls the bias current for transistor T2 and is preset to the correct value by Messrs EE Co.

R8 Increase – clockwise
R12 Increase – anti-clockwise

Train-heat voltage detector unit CU7

This unit consists simply of a bridge rectifier unit, series resistances and suppression components.

A bridge rectifier is used so that the unit will also detect AC voltages, which may be applied to coaching stock from shore supplies. The series resistances limit the current which could flow in the event of short circuit of the diodes or relay. Resistance R5 ensures that some current still flows if the relay coil becomes open-circuit or is disconnected. This means that there will always be a volt drop across resistances R1 and R4 and therefore, the full train-heat voltage is not applied to the diodes.

The capacitor acts as a suppressor for the relay coil.

Appendix 7

Testing electronic equipment

Class 50 locomotives D400–D449, April 1971

The following lists are intended to give a guide to fault-finding. It must be appreciated that only faults associated with electronic equipment are listed.

■ **Traction overloads**

Carry out the following tests 1, 2, 4, 6, 8.
Also test the KV10 for lock-on and measure the voltages between terminals 6, 7 and 8 on the KV10.

■ **High current**

Carry out the following tests 1, 2, 4, 5, 6.
Also test the field divert unit (CU2).

■ **Low current**

Carry out the following tests 1, 2, 3, 4, 5, 11.
Also test the KV10 for correct operation and the field divert unit.

■ **Low power**

Carry out the following tests 1, 2, 4, 5, 6, 8, 11.

■ **Engine shutdown**

Carry out the following test 2.
Also check the train-heat voltage at maximum rpm and the setting of HOVR.
Check the earth connection between terminal bars and check the auxiliary generator voltage when the battery charge current is less than 50A.
Check train-heat KV10 for lock-on.
Change OVR, AVR and train-heat KV10 plug-in boards in turn.

■ **Dynamic brake current high**

Carry out tests 1, 9, 10.
Also check the connections to the R13, R23 and DBP resistors.

■ **Dynamic brake current low**

Carry out tests 1, 9, 10.
Also check the connections to the R13, R23 and DBP resistors and test the dynamic brake resistors for continuity.

Testing the main control system

1 POWER SUPPLY

♦ Start the engine and check that the auxiliary generator voltage is present between terminals P40 (POS) and N on the CU1.

♦ Select EO and measure the voltage between PR (POS) and 29, and 29 (POS) and N, using a model 8 AVO set to the 25V DC range.

♦ Select FOR and re-check the voltage between 29 (POS) and N.

♦ Repeat test (c) from the other cab.
These voltages should be between 20V and 24V and should not vary by more than 0.25V for each of the above tests.

Voltage readings of zero or more than 24V are normally an indication of Zener diode failure.

Voltage readings in the range 10–19V are normally caused by a partial short circuit potentiometer.

2 POWER DELAY

Isolate all motors and connect a link between 6 and 6K on motor contactor interlock. Connect an AVO model 8 between terminals 13 (POS) and 6 on the main generator KV10 (100V DC range).

With the engine running the voltage should be 4–7V.

Select FOR or REV and move master handle to Position 1. After approximately 4 seconds the voltage should begin to rise, taking a further 8 seconds to rise SMOOTHLY to 30–38V.

NOTE: These times are typical only.

This tests the CA1 amplifier and the power delay circuit.

Connect the meter to terminals 2 (POS) and 3 on the main generator KV10 and repeat the tests. The voltage at this point should be zero when the master handle is at 0, rising to 4–7V, approximately ½ second after the handle is moved to position 1, and taking a further 8 seconds to rise smoothly to 85–100 volts.

This tests the main generator KV10.

3 CURRENT SETTING AND CURRENT LIMIT

Isolate all motors, start engine, connect AVO 8 between terminals 29 (POS) and T on CU1. Check that current limit is set on maximum. Carry out the following tests:

Select FOR or REV – the meter should read less than 2V.

Move master handle to notch 7 – the meter should read 5.5 to 6.2V.

Move current limit slowly to minimum. The voltage should fall smoothly to less than 1V.

Repeat tests from other cab.

4 DIVERT SETTING SIGNAL
Engine Running T/Motors Isolated

Measure the voltage between 29 (POS) and Z. This should be 5.4 to 5.8V.

If a zero reading is obtained, the CA2 amplifier should be changed. A fault of this nature will give loss of power after the first field divert operates (27–35mph).

A reading of 15–20V indicates an open circuit due to a defective diode or dirty or loose connections on the CA2 amplifier. The CA2 should be checked for security and changed if necessary.

A fault of this nature may give traction overloads after the first field divert operates.

5 MAXIMUM CURRENT SETTING Engine running
MCS all out. Master handle FOR or REV

Check the connections to the R15 resistor. This resistor is used to trim the maximum current of the control system.

If wire PR or the slider connection is disconnected, this will give high current and possible traction overloads.

If wire 29 is disconnected, then the current will be low.

The voltage between R15 slider and terminal 29 should be between 0 and 9V and may be set if necessary as follows.

Measure voltage between N and 29 (POS) and subtract 20V from reading. Multiply by 2.3. Connect meter between R15 slider and 29 and adjust slider to give the above value. Please note: 1 volt charge changes max current by 60 amps.

6 DCCT CIRCUIT

Connect a variable resistor of more than 200 ohms and capable of carrying 0.5A in series with an AVO (1A AC range) between terminals AD and DC1 (on DCCT 1). Close the battery switch and start the engine. Adjust resistor to give a current of 0.4A. The cab ammeters should read 800A. Measure the voltage across resistor R4. This should be 8V. Repeat the above with resistor and meter connected between AD and DC2, and AD and DC3.

Similar results should be obtained from each test.

If the above test is not correct, check that the alternator mounted on top of the fuel pump is giving an output of between 65 and 75V.

If different results are obtained for each DCCT, then a systematic check of the components associated with the DCCT circuits should be made.

The DCCT may be tested for continuity by removing one of the connections and measuring the resistance of the windings. This resistance must be between 13 and 18 ohms.

7 LOAD LIMITING POTENTIOMETER Engine running.

Connect an AVO (25V DC) between terminals LR (POS) and 29.

Operate a wheelslip relay WS1, 2, 3 by hand. The voltage should rise from less than 2V to 22V smoothly. Release the relay and the voltage should fall smoothly to less than 2V.

8 DYNAMIC BRAKE POTENTIOMETER

Disconnect cable and wire from DB4 contractor as in 1(c). Connect an AVO (25V DC range) between terminals 29 (POS) and T on the CU1. Select AIR GOODS and FOR or REV and make a 'Full service' application (Air brake off, AWS switch up). The voltage should rise smoothly from less than 1V to 3.6–4V. The actual value should be 2.2V less than the value obtained in 3(b). R23 (coarse) and R13 (fine).

9 DYNAMIC BRAKE MAXIMUM CURRENT RESISTOR

If the voltage obtained in 8 or above is incorrect, check the connections to the R23 resistor in CU1.

10 WHEELSLIP SIGNAL

Repeat test 6 but take additional voltage readings between 29 (POS) and the top of R7 (neg).

This voltage should be 5.13V to 5.18V (10V DC range), i.e. of the voltage across R4 less between 0.15 and 0.2V.

This can be adjusted if necessary by resistor R7.

Voltages significantly above 5.18V will give false wheelslip signals and loss of power. Voltages below 5.13 will not give the required wheelslip sensitivity, but will not cause loss of power.

11 TESTING SLOW-SPEED CONTROL
Preparation

♦ Isolate all traction motors and connect a link between 6 and 6K on a motor contactor coil.
♦ Disconnect the flexible cable from the axle probe.
♦ Connect the level oscillator to terminals 1 and 2 on CU10, and set to 26 hertz 100mV.
♦ Connect meter (100V DC range) to terminals 2 (POS) and 3 on the main generator KV10.
♦ Close BIS, start engine, move AWS handle up, de-isolate the brake and switch to slow speed.

Testing

♦ Move the reverser handle to FOR and note that the speedometer reads 2mph.
♦ Set slow-speed potentiometer to 1mph.
♦ Move master handle to position 3. The meter should read 4–7 volts (min field).

- ◆ Set slow-speed potentiometer to 3mph. The voltage should rise to 85–100V (max field).
- ◆ Move slow-speed potentiometer slowly towards 0mph and check that the voltage falls to min. field.

12 SLOW-SPEED SETTING POTENTIOMETERS

If test 11 is not correct, check the potentiometers as follows:

Connect an AVO (25V D-C range) between D1 and 29. Start engine and select FOR or REV. Move the slow-speed potentiometer from 0 to 3mph. The voltage should rise from 0 to 22V.

Repeat for other cab (wires D2 and 29).

13 SLOW-SPEED CONVERTER UNIT (CU11)

Connect the level oscillator as for test 11. Connect an AVO between terminals D and B on CU11 or S (POS) and 29 on CU1. Select slow speed and FOR or REV. Inject a signal of 39 c/s (3mph); the voltage should be 9 to 11V. Check at 26 and 13 c/s. The voltages should be 6 to 7V and 3 to 3.5V respectively.

The signal for this unit is obtained from tray 6 in the AEI speedometer unit (CU10) and this unit should be checked in accordance with the appropriate standing order.

Suggested methods of setting up procedures for current and load control system, Train-heat control system and HOVR.

Setting up the current and load control system

1 SETTING MAXIMUM CURRENT

- ◆ Start engine and select forward or reverse.
- ◆ Measure the voltage between terminals 29 (POS) and N (25V DC range).
- ◆ Subtract 20 from reading and multiply by 2.3.
- ◆ Adjust R15 resistor until the voltage between the slider and 29 is the same as above.

Example:

- ◆ Voltage between 29 and N is 23V, therefore R15 must be set to (23-20) 2.3 = 6.9V.

2 SETTING MAXIMUM DYNAMIC BRAKE CURRENT

- ◆ Preparation
- ◆ Disconnect cables DB4 from DB4 contactor.
- ◆ Isolate all traction motors.
- ◆ Close B15 and start engine.
- ◆ Select forward and move master handle to position 7.
- ◆ Measure the voltage between terminals 29 (POS) and T.
- ◆ Move master handle to 'Off' and switch all motors in.
- ◆ Make a full service brake application and measure the voltage between terminals 29 and T again.
- ◆ This reading should be 2.2V less than the previous one.
- ◆ If necessary, adjust R23 (coarse) or R13 (fine) to give the correct setting.

3 WHEELSLIP SENSITIVITY

- ◆ Preparation
- ◆ Connect a 200 ohms, 0.5 amp variable resistor in series with an ammeter (1A AC range) between terminals AD and DC1 on DOCT1.
- ◆ Start engine and adjust resistor to give a current of 0.4A.
- ◆ Connect a meter (10V DC range) between the slider of T7 and terminal 29. Resistor R7 should be adjusted to give a reading of 5.13 to 5.18V.

4 AMMETER ADJUSTMENTS

- ◆ Adjust resistors R10 and R12 until the cab meters read 800A with the 200 ohms resistor set to 0.4A.

Wheelslip setting

Adjust R7 until the voltage between 29+ and top of R7 = .67xVR5 - 0.36 IRMS) volts

V.R.5 = voltage across R5

I.RMS = current set to usually .4A.

Setting operating voltage of HOVR

Preparation

- ◆ Remove input unit NPE7-A6 from the train-heat KV10.
- ◆ Remove pressurising fan fuse AF2.
- ◆ Connect AVO (1,000V DC range) between HA and HAA

Setting-up

- ◆ Start engine. A meter reading of between 640 and 690V should be obtained at idling speed.
- ◆ SLOWLY open the master handle and note the voltage at which the engine shuts down. Note: the voltage must not be allowed to rise above 1,000V.
- ◆ Adjust HOVR if necessary to give an operating voltage of 930–950V.

Setting operating current of GFR

Preparation

- ◆ Disconnect wire F from terminal 13 on the main generator field supply unit.
- ◆ Isolate all traction motors and connect a link between wires 6 and 6K on a motor contactor interlock.
- ◆ Connect a 150A shunt in series with GF8 wire on the GFR coil.
- ◆ Connect a potentiometer between terminals 6 and 8 on the main generator field supply unit. The potentiometer slider should be connected to terminal 13.
- ◆ Close BIS and start engine. Select forward and move master handle to position 1. Turn the potentiometer and note the current required to energise GFR. Adjust if necessary to give an operating current of 112A.

Setting up train heat

The following settings are required when the plug-in boards or complete field supply unit is changed on the train heat:

Preparation

♦ Connect a lead between cable HP and negative.
♦ Remove KV10 input unit NPE6-A7 and re-connect with extension lead.
♦ Disconnect wire E or E3 from Z69 resistor.
♦ Connect AVO (1,000V D-C range) between HA and HAA (Thin man's).
♦ Turn R8 fully anti-clockwise then clockwise two turns. Turn R12 fully clockwise then anti-clockwise two turns. Note: If the pressurising fan fuse is removed, relay PFR should be wedged in.

Setting-up

♦ Start engine and adjust resistor R8 to give 450–500V at idling speed.
♦ Press and hold the train-heat button (to apply a positive earth fault) and adjust R12 to give a drop of 30V. Voltage rises approx. 120–135V due to engine rpm.
♦ Increase engine rpm to maximum and adjust R8 to give 850V.
♦ Press and hold the train-heat button and note the drop in voltage. The voltage should fall to 800–810V. Trim R12 and R8 if necessary.
♦ Reduce the engine rpm to idling and check that the voltage falls to 640–690V.

The following are suggestions for quickly clearing a fault when the locomotive is in traffic or on a test run.

♦ *Observe the vane motor*
When accelerating from rest on full power (position 7) the vane motor should remain in the engine underloaded position up to approximately 15mph. If the vane motor moves before 10mph then an engine fault is indicated.

♦ *Sudden loss of power*
If a sudden loss of power occurs, observe the vane motor. A clockwise movement of the vane motor will at the same time as the loss of power, indicate an engine fault.
Normally the vane motor will only move one third of its maximum travel to control the engine loading.

♦ *Wheelslip*
If false wheelslip signals are suspected, disconnect wire W2 from the CU1. This will isolate the DCCT wheelslip signal.

♦ *Current limit*
Defective current-limit potentiometers can be isolated by disconnecting wire Y1 for cab 1 or Y2 for cab 2 on the CU1.

Testing slow-speed control

♦ Connect link between 6 and 6K on motor contactor interlocks.
♦ Isolate all T/M.
♦ Disconnect cable from axle probe.
♦ Connect the oscillator to terminals 1 and 3 on the AEI speedometer. Set to 26 cls – 100mV.
♦ Connect AVO to terminals 2 (POS) and 3 on the field supply unit (set to 100V DC range).
♦ Close B1S – start engine – AWS – brake.
♦ Switch to 'Slow speed'.
♦ Select 'Forward' – speedometer should read 2mph.
♦ Set slow-speed control to 1.5mph and move master handle to 3. Meter should read 4–7V (min field).
♦ Move slow-speed control to 2.5mph. Meter reading should increase to 85 to 95V. (Max field).

Index